HAVANA

*Havana grew from a straggle of huts
into the most brilliant metropolis of the
Caribbean. The city was colonized, fortified,
blown up, burned down, rebuilt, coveted
and occupied. The beautiful buildings of La
Habana Vieja as it stands today tell the
story of this remarkable city and its people.*

Photographs by Martin Charles

JULIET BARCLAY

HA

VANA

PORTRAIT OF A CITY

Foreword by Eusebio Leal Spengler

Introduction by Francisco de Borbón y Escasany

CASSELL

A CASSELL BOOK

First published in the UK 1993 by Cassell
Villiers House, 41/47 Strand, London WC2N 5JE

Format copyright © Cassell
Text copyright © 1993 Juliet Barclay
Photographs copyright © 1993 Martin Charles

Distributed in the United States by
Sterling Publishing Co., Inc.
387 Park Avenue South, New York, NY 10016–8810

Distributed in Australia by
Capricorn Link (Australia) Pty Ltd
P.O. Box 665, Lane Cove, NSW 2066

British Library Cataloguing-in-Publication Data
A catalogue record for this book is available from
the British Library

ISBN 0-304-34284-X

for Robert Williamson

The author is particularly grateful to: EUSEBIO LEAL SPENGLER

and would also like to thank: María de los Ángeles Flórez
Roberto de Armas
Eugenio Avila Bacaro
Diana Barreras Gutiérrez
Esperanza Bastaldo
Daniel Bejerano Millán
José Antonio Caballero
Francisco Canosa Montoro
Humberto Durán
Dieneke Ferguson
José Ramón Fernández
Oscar Fernández Mell
Nelson de la Fuente Diego
Alina Gaute
Bruce Gilmour
Gladys Giraldo
Maximino Gómez Alvarez
Sergio González Cias
Ramón Guerra Díaz
Omar Hastie Suárez
Zoila Lapique Becali
Alberto Lauro
María Eugenia Martín Eyia
Miguel Martínez Moles
Lesbia Méndez Vargas
Irma Pardo Olive
José Payán Flores
Tom Pocock
Aurora Amarilis Rodríguez Savigne
Marcos Rodríguez Villamil
Ricardo Rodríguez
Christine de Roo
Raúl Sánchez Abreu
Laritza Simeón Armada
Rayda Mara Suárez Portal
Lesley Thomas
Olga Lidia Triana Prieto
Niurka Varona
Publicitur
and the staff of the British Library

CONTENTS

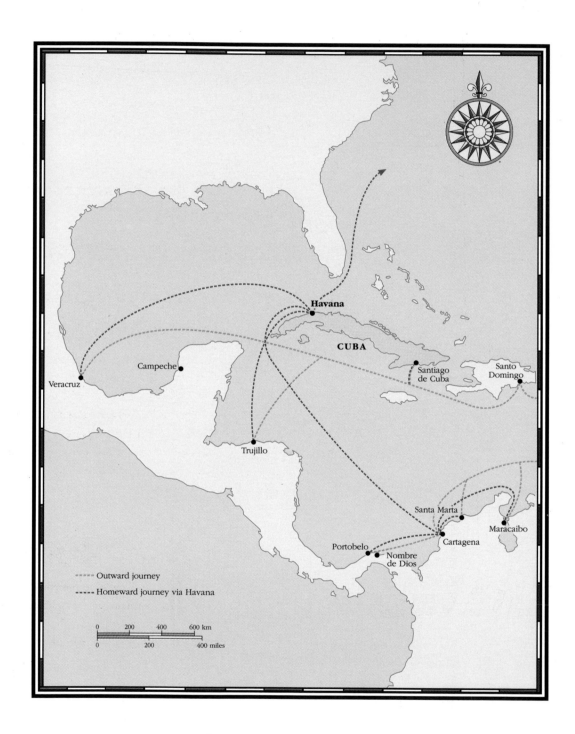

The route followed by the fleets that sailed between Spain and the Indies.

Below: Street map of Old Havana.

Right: Havana's castles.

Addresses in Havana are given with the street onto which a building faces being mentioned first, followed by the two streets that cross that street on either side of the block in which the building stands e.g. Calle Muralla No. 107, between Calle San Ignacio and Calle Inquisidor. This is most useful, especially when the numbering system in the street becomes eccentric.

SURNAMES

It is useful to remember that Spanish surnames are a combination of the first surname of the person's father, which comes first, and their mother's first surname, which comes second. Thus the daughter of María Herrera Fernández and Juan Menéndez Millán would be called Juanita Menéndez Herrera. Women's surnames remain the same after marriage.

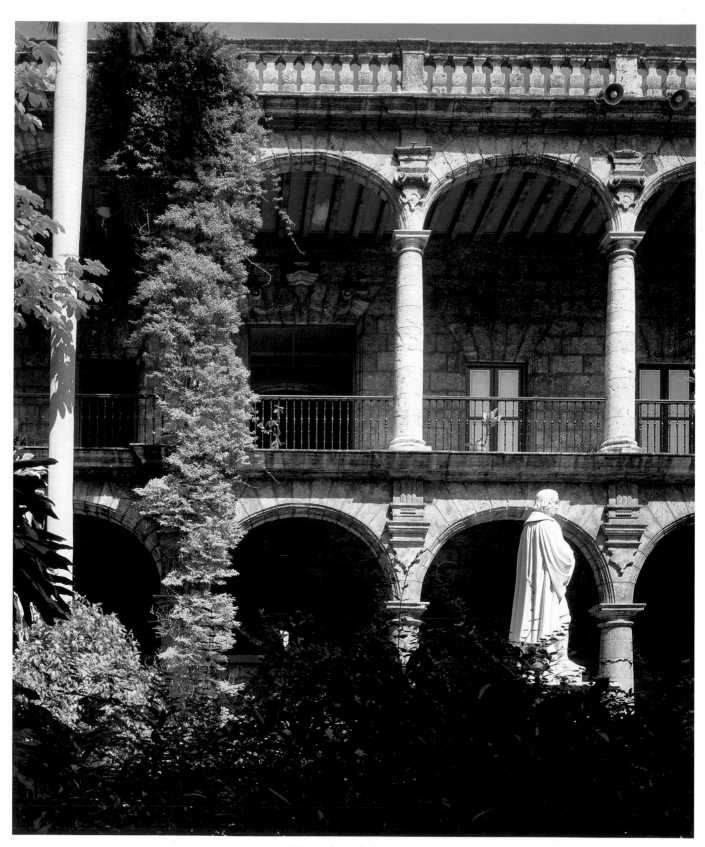

The Palacio de los Capitanes Generales (the Museum of the City of Havana).

FOREWORD

Oficina del Historiador de la Ciudad
Museo de la Habana
Palacio de los Capitanes Generales
Plaza de Armas

J uliet Barclay has visited Havana on numerous occasions, and she has always shown a discerning interest in the city, motivated essentially by the beauty of its architecture and also by her discovery of its unique history. She has taken careful note of both and has given voice to her research in several public forums in the United Kingdom. There are already numerous specialists, artists and restorers in Great Britain who are interested in the work of conservation and restoration of the historical core of the capital of Cuba, and this is due in great measure to the articles written by Juliet Barclay, especially the one published in *The Architect's Journal* in December 1990 under the title 'Havana Renaissance', which was illustrated with beautiful photographs taken by Martin Charles.

She now offers us a complete book, *Havana – Portrait of a City*, which will be included in its own right among the works of other famous women who travelled to the Caribbean, such as Amelia Murray, Maria Nugent, Fanny Erskine, Mathilde Houston and the Countess of Merlín, whose testimonies have been collated in one volume by the Cuban essayist and writer Nara Araujo.

I should also state that Juliet Barclay, like her predecessors, from necessity includes many personal impressions in her writing, but these, far from reducing the validity of her work, succeed in striking a candid note from which I would not wish to detract by inserting a single correction into the text.

I have heard the echo of other voices among her lines. She has read the classic Cuban writers and historians of Havana – José Martín Pérez de Arrate, José María de la Torre and Irene Wright – and taking these and many others by the hand, she has arrived in our own times.

May the worth of this book be duly acknowledged by the reader; may it become useful to both the English and the Spanish-speaking worlds as a new profile of our city; and may the author receive the well-deserved affection of the people of Havana.

EUSEBIO LEAL SPENGLER
Historian of the City of Havana

INTRODUCTION

Francisco de Borbón y Escasany
Duque de Sevilla

W hen Juliet Barclay contacted me requesting that I write an introduction to her book, *Havana – Portrait of a City*, I remembered stories I had heard about the daily life of that city from my paternal grandmother, who had lived there as a child when her father, the Duke of Seville, had been Governor of the island. Those were colonial times, when the heady winds of independence were not yet blowing over Cuba.

Those stories, narrated during my childhood in the 1940s and 1950s, spoke of opulence and riches, of great houses and grand balls. They conjured up a world far removed from the poverty in which we then lived in Spain, a country which had endured three years of civil war, the impossibility of economic recovery during World War II, and the isolation and blockade imposed by the Allies.

I also remember well when our Cuban cousins arrived in Madrid from Havana. They were laden with gifts which were undreamt of in Spain, as a result of import restrictions arising from a shortage of foreign reserves and the disastrous command economy which prevailed in those years.

Later, when I was President of a bank in Miami during the years 1979 to 1984, I immersed myself in the large Cuban community and re-encountered my relatives and their old stories of Havana, with which I breakfasted and dined for five unforgettable years. It was then that I learned that my ancestors had arrived in Havana as army officers at the beginning of the sixteenth century, and that by the end of the nineteenth century three of them had become military governors of the island of Cuba.

It was for all of these reasons that I immediately accepted the proposal to write an introduction to this book, although it is an introduction which, of necessity, will have to be rather modest; I am an economist and banker and thus hardly a writer. Nevertheless, I do know how difficult it must have been to compose this historical document, since I dedicated myself to historical research during my early years at the School of Economics at the University of Madrid.

Juliet Barclay's book opens with the first Spanish settlement on the original site of San Cristóbal de La Habana and its eventual move to the present location of what would become Havana. One reads these early chapters with a sense of anticipation induced by their direct and elegant style, with a certain air of mystery, which characterizes a good novel.

The history of the early colonists is filled with heroic deeds and also with brutality. As to this latter element, which undoubtedly existed, the reader should be reminded that the Spanish conquistador of the sixteenth century, at the dawn of the Renaissance, was a man of his times, with passions, vices and, perhaps, a certain religious fanaticism, but also charged with ideals and a sense of the universality of life. In general, he was also imbued with great courage. If the deeds of the Spanish conquistador are compared with those of other European colonists two and three centuries later, one notes that, in the majority of cases, the conquistador emerges as having been more moderate. It should also be recalled that the 'Laws of the Indies', which were proclaimed by King Ferdinand and Queen Isabella at the end of the fifteenth century, provided a legal framework for the tolerance and defence of native interests. Alas, they were not always followed, regardless of the zeal in their application exercised by some of the clergy.

The book maintains its exciting tempo when historical references give way to customs, anecdotes, cultural elements and a description of the principal buildings and monuments of Old Havana.

I would like to emphasize the enormous investigative task which Juliet Barclay undertook in order to write this book, a task which was undoubtedly assisted by the great love of bureaucracy which has always burned in the breast of the Spanish civil servant. Writers, chroniclers and scriveners have captured in detail all the events of their times in both Spain and the New World, putting to shame their European counterparts who have by comparison left historical voids, even well into the nineteenth century.

To end this brief introduction, I would like to congratulate Juliet Barclay for her great work, of which this fine book is the consummate result. I have no doubt that it will become a necessary work of reference to future students of the history of Havana.

FRANCISCO DE BORBON Y ESCASANY
Duke of Seville

1
DISCOVERERS AND EXPLORERS

'One of these provinces is called Avan, and there the people are born with tails.'

Christopher Columbus[1]

IN THE PALE EARLY LIGHT THE ancient buildings in the Plaza de Armas have the grey sheen of pewter and the paving stones feel smooth and cold. As the enormous orange sun lifts from the hills behind the harbour the walls and columns glow, and the brightness blinds the lighthouse's small eye.

For the first settlers of Havana the rising sun brought the relief of having survived another dark, frightening night. Their days were almost as uncertain. Driven by adventurous self-confidence coupled with fierce faith and the gleaming dream of El Dorado, they battled with fever, Indians, pirates and meagre resources to build a home from home on the geographical and spiritual edge of an unknown future.

Christopher Columbus found Cuba green, luscious, scented, dripping with fruit and ringing with bird-song on 28 October 1492. He exclaimed that 'this island is the most beautiful that eyes have ever seen'.[2] He was, however, apt in his enthusiasm to inflate one-off experiences, vague hints and second-hand stories into certainties. As he approached Cuba's shores he was convinced that the island was Cathay, that merchant ships swarmed about its coast and that inland lay the great city of Hangchow and the abode of the all-powerful Great Khan, surrounded by rocks and rivers that glittered with gold.

No doubt it was very difficult for Columbus to resist exploring the island himself. He was entranced by his new

The Castillo de la Real Fuerza in the Plaza de Armas, at dawn.

discovery. After taking a boat up the river where he had anchored, he said that he could hardly bear to leave all the strange and beautiful vegetation and the sound of the birds singing to return to his ship. However, he wisely thought that a large landing party might terrify the natives, so he chose two of his men and sent them off to explore the interior. He told them to be friendly and polite to anyone that they met.

Eight days later the expedition returned, full of strange tales. They had found a large village of round huts. The Indians who lived there, delighted with the arrival of bearded and beribboned apparitions speaking an unintelligible language, had hoisted them onto their shoulders and carried them in state to their own special hut. It was furnished with wooden seats ingeniously carved in the shapes of animals with four paws, tails and, best of all, golden eyes and ears.

The Cuban Indians were gentle, generous and unsuspecting, experts at making pottery and polished stone implements. They lived in modest settlements, hunted, fished and grew beans and maize. The fastidious Spaniards related with horrified fascination that they supplemented their diet with spiders and grubs and smoked 'perfumed herbs'[3] (tobacco), ignited with live coals which they carried around with them.

The Indians decided that the best explanation for the appearance of the exotic and unsuitably dressed strangers was that they had dropped from the sky. One by one they solemnly kissed the Spaniards' hands and feet. They showered them with presents, fed them on sweet potatoes and begged them to stay. The Great Khan was conspicuous by his absence, however, and the sweet potatoes palled. When their hosts told the Spaniards that gold, pearls and spices could be found in large quantities in a land to the east, they decided to return to their ships. A few of the Indians went with them. Their fellows were left behind with no inkling that they had welcomed into their midst the vanguard of the force that was to exterminate them in the space of a century.

For several years afterwards the avaricious Spanish gaze shifted to other islands, but in 1509 King Ferdinand gave Diego Columbus, Christopher's son, the title of Governor of the Indies and told him to organize further exploration of Cuba. To head the expedition on his behalf, Diego Columbus chose Diego Velázquez de Cuellar. Velázquez was a distinguished soldier, handsome, blonde, swashbuckling and popular, but most importantly he was rich enough to defray the costs of the expedition. He sailed to Cuba in November 1511

Opposite: A sixteenth-century map of the island of Cuba.

Above left: Diego Velázquez de Cuellar.

Above right: The Cuban Indians smoked rolls of tobacco leaves which they called *cohibas*.

with thirty men, a mixture of impoverished Spanish noblemen and ex-convicts who had been freed and given the dubious privilege of colonizing the New World.

Velázquez also took with him a priest called Bartolomé de las Casas. When de las Casas saw the manner in which the Indians were treated by the Spaniards he was horrified; later he was to write:

> One time the Indians came to meete us, and to receive us with victuals, and delicate cheere… they presented us with a great quantity of fish, and of bread, and other meate, together with all that they could doe for us to the uttermost. See incontinent the Devill, which put himselfe into the Spaniards, to put them all to the edge of the sword in my presence, without any cause whatsoever, more than three thousand soules, which were set before us, men, women and children. I saw there so great cruelties, that never any man living either have or shall see the like.[4]

18   Bartolomé de las Casas.

In 1511, however, the explorers met with opposition in Cuba. A far-sighted Indian chief named Hatuey had been whipping up resentment of the Spaniards among his people. The Indians made a valiant yet naive attempt to repel the invaders, but their primitive weapons were no match for Velázquez's experience and superior resources. Hatuey was captured and burned at the stake. As the flames crackled around his feet he was offered the chance of conversion to Christianity and the opportunity of going to heaven. He asked whether there were Christians there, and on being assured that this was so, replied that he had no desire to be in any place where there were people as cruel as the Spaniards; he would rather go to hell.

The death of Hatuey.

A sixteenth-century map of Havana.

2

SETTLERS – THE BIRTH OF A CITY

'I have not yet seen any signs of the rich mines with which our imaginations have been deluded.'

Hernando de la Parra[1]

ATUEY'S HEROIC stand had been little more than a temporary inconvenience to the invading Spaniards. Diego Velázquez pressed on with his determined programme of acquisition and domination. He ordered the establishment of seven settlements, one of which was called San Cristóbal de La Habana.

This first Havana was located on the south coast of the island at Batabanó, almost opposite where the city now stands on the north side of the island. Nobody knows exactly when it was founded, as the town's records were later lost on one of the many occasions when Havana was burned to the ground by pirates. The most likely date is 25 July (St Christopher's Day) 1515. The settlement was established by Pánfilo de Narváez, one of Velázquez's men. No doubt de Narváez had excellent qualities or Velázquez, who was an experienced commander and whose personal fortune was tied up in the project, would not have chosen him for the job. Selecting sites, however, was not one of his talents. The settlement was an unqualified disaster. The coast beside it was too flat for ships to run in to the shore, the land was little more than a disease-ridden swamp, and the climate was unbearably hot and steamy.

If it had not been for the example of good humour and energy set by Velázquez, his men might quickly have abandoned Havana. But the character of their commander inspired great loyalty, and they hung on for some time. Eventually, however, the situation became intolerable. The settlers, suffering from horrible tropical ailments and plagued by voracious insects, moved to a site on the north coast at the mouth of the River Chorrera (now Almendares). When they arrived there the area was a wilderness. Now it is surrounded by one of the less distinguished parts of twentieth-century Havana. All day cars roar underneath it through a tunnel from the Malecón to Fifth Avenue. A large and sinister pipe projects into the sea. Groups of fishermen, apparently oblivious to the eye-watering smell, sit on the sea wall ignoring their lines. One does not hang around the Almendares longer than one can help, and the sixteenth-century Spaniards did not linger either. The settlers soon found a far more promising site for their settlement a few miles down the coast: a large bay with a narrow, rocky mouth surrounded by rolling hills. On 25 November 1519 they moved again, to the site of what was to become the city of San Cristóbal de La Habana.

A map showing the two locations of San Cristóbal de La Habana in the sixteenth century.

At first the site was known as Puerto de Carenas, for it was an ideal place to careen ships, and pitch for caulking could be found on the rocks by the shore. In 1538, however, it was given the same name as the old southern settlement. Although the climate and geography were an enormous improvement on the southern site, survival was still far from easy for the Spaniards. Had they been able to foresee the trials that lay ahead of them in the establishment of Havana they would probably have given up the idea without further ado. Everything required for day-to-day existence had to be imported: seed for future crops, tools to prepare the land for planting, building equipment, clothing and food. All these imports had to be paid for, and the only way to accomplish this was to use the precious time that could have been spent on building houses in overseeing the extraction of gold dust from the sand of local rivers. To make matters worse, the supplies of gold, as Alonso Parada wrote on 2 July 1527, were 'diminishing every day'.[2] Eventually the settlers turned their attention to agriculture, but they found it almost impossible to produce the quantities that they needed to survive.

The first houses built in Havana stood in a row facing the sea, between the present sites of the Plaza de Armas and the Plaza de San Francisco. The settlers had neither the time nor the resources to construct anything more ambitious than huts along the lines of the Indian *bohíos*. The walls were made of mud smoothed on in slimy layers and left to harden, and crack, in the sun. The floors were beaten earth, and the roofs were thatched, after a fashion, with palm leaves. The furniture inside the huts was primitive, consisting of crude wooden tables, splintery benches and the odd leather hammock. Meals were eaten off wooden plates, and the only real concessions to civilization were pictures of saints hung on the lumpy walls. Those who were reasonably well-off lit the interiors of their huts with lanterns filled with olive oil imported from Seville, but the less privileged majority had to make do with candles. Life was Spartan in the extreme.

While the settlers in Cuba were struggling to establish themselves, their countrymen were pressing forward into the New World. Havana's proximity to the deep channel between Cuba and the Bahamas (Baja Mar means shallow sea, and the waters around those islands are treacherous) was an enormous advantage to the growing maritime traffic between Spain and her latest acquisitions. From Cuba went the expeditions that discovered Yucatán in 1517, as well as Hernán Cortés's famous expeditions for the conquest of Mexico in 1519–21.

During the sixteenth century ships began to call into the port in ever-increasing numbers. In July 1553 it became the unofficial capital of Cuba after the governor, Gonzalo Pérez de Angulo, moved from the previous capital, Santiago de Cuba in the east of the island, to make Havana his permanent residence.

Although some of Cuba's governors general undoubtedly had the best interests of the island at heart, the careers of most of them were marked by cruelty, greed and self-aggrandisement. In 1544 the hard-pressed citizens of Havana had an early taste of these megalomaniac tendencies. Governor Juan de Ávila arrived in town from Santiago and decided to make an extended stay. The reason for this, he explained, was that French pirates were lurking off the coast and Havana would need his help to withstand any attack that they might make. De Ávila's initial good intentions were soon swallowed up by corruption and tyranny – anyone who was foolish enough to write anything negative about him was gaoled, and gossip about his iniquities even travelled to the next-door island of Hispaniola. The citizens were dismayed when it began to look as though he were planning an even longer visit. He proceeded to build himself a house on a piece of land ceded by the settlement and forced the people to donate the construction materials; muttering resentfully, they christened the building the House of Fear. When he finally returned to Santiago, to the arms of his mistress, Doña Guiomar de Guzmán, there were loud sighs of relief in Havana.

The settlement increased in importance as the new territories in South America began to yield up their riches. The quantities of treasure that were transported to Spain from the Indies were staggering. In 1503 the royal income amounted to 8,000 ducados. The figure rose to almost 59,000 in 1509, to about 90,000 in 1512 and to about 120,000 in 1518. After the conquests of Mexico and Peru the quantities soared further. The fleet of 1551 carried over a million and a half ducados, and the fleet of 1583 had to leave a million pesos behind in Havana because there was simply insufficient room in the ships' holds. In 1587 a Spanish historian wrote that there was enough New World treasure in Spain to pave the streets of Seville with blocks of gold and silver. Every year, from March to August, galleons crowded into the port of Havana. They were laden not only with gold and silver, but also with emeralds and indigo, cochineal and cocoa, pearls and vividly coloured birds' feathers. There were usually at least twenty or thirty ships in the harbour, and the royal fleet sometimes stayed there for six months at a time. From 1565 pearls, perfumes, silks and ivories also began to arrive in the town from the Pacific via Veracruz.

Cuban exports gathered momentum, and quantities of tobacco, leather, fruit and precious woods were added to the cargoes being dispatched to Seville, from where all sorts of glorious luxuries were returned: fine wines, silk ribbons and buttons, little mirrors, elaborate hats, embroideries, taffeta hangings, olives, saffron and cloth of gold. Some of the inhabitants of the town, although their houses were still very humble, began to deck themselves out in French linens and brightly coloured silks and velvets. They wore gold rings and chains, and carried swords and daggers decorated with jewels.

If you stand on the Avenida del Puerto early in the morning, before the start of another twentieth-century day's racket, while the rising sun is still gilding the surface of the water, you can half shut your eyes and imagine the great galleons slipping into the harbour, and the rich goods piled on the wharves in front of the tiny town huddled on the shore. Havana's hills are now so encrusted with buildings that they can no longer be seen, but then they were full of greenery and bird-song and curved comfortingly around the bay to which all the treasures of the New World were transported every year.

But by no stretch of the imagination could sixteenth-century Havana have been described as civilized. Nature, if not in tooth, was certainly red in claw: the settlement often became overrun with vast numbers of tortoises and crabs. At night the scrabbling and gnawing sounded like a vast army on the move. The tortoises were caught and made into *tasajo*, unappetizing strips of dried meat, which were boiled and eaten by the sailors on their voyages back to Spain. At times the revolting smell of dead tortoise permeated the entire town. By 1590 the production of *tasajo* for provisioning the galleons had reached fever pitch and the stench had become unbearable. The town council decreed that the animals should only be killed outside the settlement 'because of the danger to health and the unpleasant smell of their remains'.[3]

Havana's increasing commercial activity and wealth and the corresponding necessity for agricultural development resulted in an urgent need for labour. By the middle of the sixteenth century the native population of the island had been almost wiped out, either swiftly by the sword or more slowly by hard labour and new European diseases. A new type of cargo began to enter Havana's port, and the trickle of shipments soon turned into a flood.

Although these goods did not last for very long after their arrival, they were abundant and cheap, and as long as the holds were packed to capacity, each voyage made an excellent profit. The lucrative new cargo was human.

The arrival of African slaves in Cuba marked the start of three centuries of suffering and of one of the most significant influences on the island's cultural development. They were immediately set to work for little or no reward, and any efforts that they made to augment their income were frowned upon. In June 1551 the town council decreed:

> It is reported that Negro workers are collecting... grapes... and oranges... their masters are thus inconvenienced by their slaves becoming idle... it is thus publicly proclaimed that no Negro labourer may sell oranges nor bananas nor grapes nor any other fruits, nor may any other Negro who is not a labourer sell such items. If they are found in possession of such objects intending to sell them they will incur the penalty of three hundred lashes given publicly in the open streets of this town and ten days in prison, chained in the stocks.[4]

As the town began to fill regularly with shiploads of sailors looking for a good time before the long voyage home, the moral standards of the inhabitants of Havana, already less than exalted, took a steep dive. At first, the citizens never ventured out of their houses at night unless they were heavily armed. In addition to crabs, runaway slaves and packs of savage dogs all hunting for food, the streets were full of drunken mariners making the most of their shore leave. But the rot began to spread, and since more cultivated entertainments were few and far between, the people took to drinking far too much and gambling with gold bars, emeralds and pearls. During the town council meeting on 18 April 1551 the fact that 'the inns of this town are very disorderly'[5] was lamented, and later it was declared that 'since there is so much disorder on Sundays and festive days due to the inns selling wine and food before mass it is publicly ordered that no innkeeper may open his establishment or sell wine to anybody until after church'[6].

Frightful penalties were also introduced for swearing:

> Any soldier who while gambling or in general conversation speaks ill of our Lord or our Lady or the Saints will be placed in the stocks for thirty days as decreed by law, and the second time for another thirty days... and on the third disgraceful occasion he will be condemned to row in the galleys for four years, as a blasphemer and a bad Christian.[7]

It was galling for the citizens of Havana to see the enormous riches, from which they received few benefits, passing so briefly under their noses *en route* to Spain. The town had become little more than an inadequate service station for galleons, and it was physically unable to cope with the enormous influxes of people from the fleets. On 31 May 1545 Governor Juan de Ávila wrote to the king:

> In this town of Havana there is a pressing necessity to supply water to the large numbers of ships that arrive here, and so many sailors, black slaves and Indians die that we beg Your Majesty to issue a royal decree that every ship that enters this port pays a tariff for every ton of goods and every slave that it carries in order that we may construct a wharf from which to supply the said water.[8]

Most of the inhabitants of the town were poor, but any attempts that they made to rectify the situation were swiftly nipped in the bud by the town council.

> In as much as the provisions, bread, fruit and other vegetables for sale in this town are being sold secretly to the detriment of the republic, it is decreed that whatsoever person, Spanish, black or Indian, who intends to sell provisions such as bread and fruit and other vegetables must sell them in the public places of this town and not in their houses in secret, on pain, if they are Spanish, of confiscation of the goods they are selling and a fine of three ducados....
>
> If any black man or woman or Indian man or woman commits the said crime and has not the means to pay the fine they will receive one hundred lashes on the public streets for the first offence and this will be doubled for the second offence and trebled for the third and they will be banished from this town for one year.[9]

Not surprisingly, the restrictions and pressures on the townspeople caused eruptions of rage and resentment, seasoned with a liberal dash of tale-telling. In the 1580s a bitter row blew up between Gabriel de Luján, the governor general, and Captain Diego Fernández de Quiñones, the mayor of Havana and commander of the castle, after de Luján had repeatedly tried to overturn official decisions made by Fernández de Quiñones. The mayor wrote to the king in December 1582:

> I have heard it from the governor's own lips that he has 16,000 ducados in Spain... he has a great quantity of pearls that I have seen with my own eyes and his wife has declared publicly that he has earned 4,000 ducados in rents in two years, which would not be an unreasonable profit for this job if it were legal.[10]

In his turn, de Luján wrote to the king in December 1584:

> Under the obligations of the position that I hold and in order to disburden my conscience I am bound to inform Your Majesty that the mayor and his sergeant and second lieutenant are parading three married women in public as though they were their own wives.[11]

The argument grew until it assumed the proportions of a public scandal, and finally, in December 1588, an exasperated decree arrived from the king in which the official positions of the protagonists in the affair were merged into one:

> In as much as I have noted the discords and differences which exist between Gabriel de Luján, my governor of the island of Cuba, and Diego Fernández de Quiñones, my captain and mayor of the fortress of Havana, and the inconveniences and damages which have resulted from this and may yet result, I have decided that in the said island there will be only one person in whom the power in all matters of government, war and justice will reside... Field Marshal Juan de Tejeda, Knight of the Order of Santiago, whom I have declared to be my governor of the said island of Cuba.[12]

The population of Havana was still small in the last quarter of the century. In 1582 it included only 276 Spaniards and 50 Indians, but by the mid-1500s, buildings had begun to spread northwards towards the edge of the bay outside the main harbour. By the end of the century the town had several streets, the configuration of which set the style for the future development of the city. While their extreme narrowness provided much-needed shade for most of the day it became a curse as urban traffic increased. The street names give a fair idea of the townspeople's way of life. Calle Real (Royal Street, now Calle Muralla), Mercaderes (merchants), Oficios (craftsmen) and Redes (nets, now Calle Inquisidor) are encouraging, but Sumidero (sewer, now Calle O'Reilly) and Basurero (rubbish dump, now Calle Teniente Rey) speak for themselves. These last two are now among Havana's most important streets, clicking every morning with the purposeful heels of well-pressed crowds on their way to work. No doubt in the sixteenth century they would have been avoided like the plague.

Although construction was actively pursued throughout the century, stone was seldom used, but wood and tiles were being added to the basic materials of mud and thatch. There is one house dating from around 1570 still standing in Havana. It is in Calle Obispo, at number 117–119. Although it has been extensively altered over the centuries, its simple layout, with

Calle Obispo 117–119, built in the late sixteenth century.

living quarters upstairs and slave quarters downstairs, is characteristic of the period.

The style of two other houses, one on the corner of Calles Teniente Rey and Bernaza and the other on the corner of Calles Paula and Habana, is also of the sixteenth century. Since this area of the town was not developed at that time it is possible that they were farmhouses built outside the boundaries of the settlement. Neither of them has been significantly altered since their construction.

Havana, though now firmly established as a town, was still lacking in culture and many of its inhabitants remained woefully uncouth. An attempt at civilized entertainment was made in 1598 on the saint's day of Governor Juan Maldonado with the first theatrical presentation to be put on in Havana. It was a comedy, performed on a special stage erected near the walls of the castle, with the unpromising title *The Good People in Heaven and the Bad People on Earth*. For some time the audience was singularly unappreciative of this cultural offering, chattering continually in loud voices throughout the performance. Governor Maldonado fumed silently at their boorish behaviour. His saint's day was being spoiled. Finally he could bear it no longer and burst out in menacing tones that if they did not have the grace to be quiet they could look forward to a spell in the stocks. At this everyone not only subsided but conceived an exaggerated passion for the entertainment. Although the play did not finish until one o'clock in the morning, they all protested that it was too marvellous and insisted that the unfortunate actors start again at the beginning.

What the settlers may have lacked in social graces was made up for by their tenacity. The sixteenth century drew to a close with official royal recognition of the tremendous strategic importance and potential of Havana:

Don Felipe, by the grace of God, King of Castile, of León, of Aragón … in consideration that the citizens and inhabitants of the town of San Cristóbal de La Habana in the island of Cuba have served me in its defence and resistance against enemies, and as the said town is among the principal settlements of the said island where my governor and officials of my estate reside I wish to ennoble and enlarge it. I therefore desire and decree that from now and henceforth·for ever the said town will be entitled City of San Cristóbal de La Habana of the said island of Cuba.[13]

A sixteenth-century house at the corner of Calles Habana and Paula.

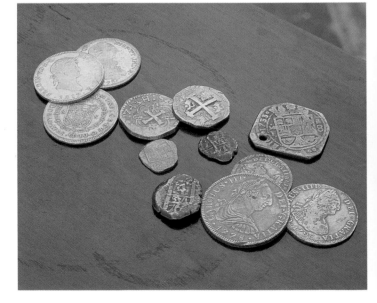

3

PIRATES AND PRIVATEERS

They called a Council; and some were of opinion, 'twere convenient to assault the City of Havana, under the obscurity of night. Which Enterprize, they said, might easily be performed; especially if they could but take any few of the Ecclesiasticks, and make them Prisoners. Yea, that the City might be sack'd, before the Castles could put themselves in a posture of defence.

Captain Henry Morgan's crew consider an attack on Havana – Alexander Olivier Exquemeling[1]

Spanish treasure...

Above left: A seventeenth-century solid gold plate.

Above right: A silver gilt salt cellar *c.* 1600.

Below left: A pectoral cross set with seven Colombian emeralds.

Below right: Pieces of eight: escudo and real coins.

Pictures top and below left courtesy of the Mel Fisher Maritime Heritage Society. Photographer: Dylan Kibler.

I T WAS ALL VERY WELL TO GIVE IT the grandiose title of a city, but sixteenth-century Havana had few of the airs and graces that the term implies. Scruffy, dirty, smelly, dusty in the sun, squelching with rancid mud when it rained, it clung chaotically to the shore. The people's priorities were basic. Food, water, shelter and the struggle for survival distracted their attention from the fact that they were sitting on a fortune. It simply did not occur to them that eyes might be focusing on Havana from a dangerous direction. The Habaneros were in for a horrid shock. The problems of basic survival were about to pale into insignificance before a far more frightening prospect. Elsewhere sails were being set and a different type of craft was bearing inexorably down upon them – pirates!

Havana was a treasure chest, and nobody had thought to lock the lid. The galleons in the harbour were very low in the water and it was clear why: their holds were tightly packed with enough treasure for everyone in the town to retire several times over. It was impossible to hide the fact, even if the Habaneros had known who to hide it from. Every time another ship's crew swaggered into town the streets became crowded with strangers and it was impossible to distinguish friend from foe. The voyages from Spain to the Caribbean were long, boring and uncomfortable, and many of the sailors were driven to undertake them only by the desire for treasure. There was really not much to choose from between the toughs who crewed the official ships and the pirates and informers who were able to saunter around Havana's streets at their leisure, memorizing the layout of the town and calculating the value of the goods in the port. Sometimes they wore disguises, rendering their detection almost impossible.

The pirates acquired their intelligence carefully. Some of them were professional privateers licensed by the monarchs of Spain's European competitors to harry and plunder her shipping and ports; others were individual opportunists. All of them were ruthless.

The Habaneros were inadequately armed and utterly terrified. Pirate stories were constantly circulated. The crews of incoming ships would relate tales·of merciless attack and gory death on the high seas. Every time a sail was sighted on the horizon a frisson of fear ran through the city. As a ship came closer the people, crowding together in anxious groups on the wharves, would squint desperately in the sun to try to identify it. They were all too well aware that they were an easy target. One day in 1538 the speck became a sail, the sail became a vessel, then two, then the voices of the crews could be heard ringing out over the water... they were speaking French!

The people scrambled into their houses and barred the doors, watching for the shadows of feet moving back and forth outside. But mud and thatch might have been paper for all the good it did in keeping out marauders. These French pirates simply set fire to a few buildings as a foretaste of what might happen if the Habaneros did not agree to their terms. The palm thatch, wood and pitch went up like tinder, blackening and crackling, the flames almost invisible in the bright light, and the smoke clouding the sun.

The Habaneros counted out 600 ducados. The pirates, greatly satisfied with a fee so easily earned, retired to their ships and sailed away. Everyone in Havana was burning with indignation, but having had an example of what the pirates were capable of they were reluctant to give chase. Then, however, Spanish sails were sighted, and with them came an opportunity for revenge. As soon as the three ships anchored, the admiral in command was besieged with

Opposite and above: French pirates attacking
Havana and the surrounding settlements.

35

descriptions of the pirates and instructions to follow them. The ships' cargoes of gold and silver were hastily unloaded, the muttering crews hoisted the sails, and they went off in unenthusiastic pursuit.

They found the French soon enough, at anchor in the mouth of a river. It was too soon for the admiral's liking, for the other two ships were lagging behind and he was loath to face the unprincipled ruffians by himself. The ruffians, however, were flushed with their success and wanted more sport. They opened fire. The admiral's nerves failed him, and without firing a single shot he changed course and promptly ran aground. He may not have done it on purpose, but he and the crew were past caring. They scuttled ashore as fast they could. The second and third ships had caught up by this time, but when they saw their colleagues' lily-livered behaviour they, too, panicked and turned tail and fled.

The pirates were delighted and agreed that if this was the degree of opposition that they could expect from Havana they had underpitched their first demand. Back they sailed to the city. The despairing inhabitants produced another 600 ducados. However, if they thought that would satisfy the pirates they were much mistaken. The latter, with their pockets chinking with coins, enjoyed fifteen days' looting and pillaging. They combed the city for every movable item of any value and even took the church bells. As a final gesture of contempt they hung an image of St Peter on the door of one of the houses and pelted it with oranges.

Something obviously had to be done to strengthen Havana's defences. Governor Hernando de Soto gave orders for the construction of the first Castillo de la Real Fuerza. This could protect the city from the seaward side, but the news travelled fast along the Caribbean grapevine that Havana was still vulnerable to landward. The tidings encouraged an English pirate to chance his luck. He landed along the coast from the city, moved inland and entered Havana before dawn with the greatest of ease. The Habaneros, waking to find pirates in their midst, decided this time that discretion was definitely the better part of valour. Running into the woods as fast as they were able, they hid in the undergrowth while the pirates ransacked the town without hindrance.

By the middle of the sixteenth century everyone in Havana was in a constant state of anxiety. Their sleepless nights were made yet more agonizing by a decree that prohibited anyone from ever taking his sword off.

In July 1555 another corsair arrived. He was a Frenchman called Jacques de Sores, who had acquired a comprehensive training in the piratical arts. By the time he bore down upon the miserable citizens of Havana he had become so famous (or infamous) for his fiendish skills that he had received royal patronage, both from the French and from Elizabeth of England.

On the morning of 10 July the lookout on the heights of the Morro above the harbour mouth saw an approaching sail. As quickly as he could he displayed the appropriate signal. The guard in the fort of the Fuerza repeated it to place the city on the alert. The usual harrowing pause ensued, but all too soon the Habaneros realized that it was not one ship but two, and that they were French caravels. Horror and dismay spread through the city. Although it was true that Havana now had a fort, its name, Castle of the Royal Force, was over-optimistic. The pirate de Sores had gained information from a Portuguese pilot who had recently visited the port and knew that the castle's ability to protect Havana was a tale to be told to children and not to any self-respecting buccaneer. The Habaneros probably knew that the situation looked pretty hopeless from the outset. There were only a hundred men available to fight, and some of them hardly counted as they were old or ill. The armaments were in an equally sorry state. Apart from the odd weapon owned by individual citizens, there were only thirty functioning harquebuses in the city and hardly any ammunition. This time, however, the Habaneros resolved to make an attempt to save their homes, their honour and their lives.

The commander of the Fuerza, Juan de Lobera, organized the pathetic force into some semblance of order. Then someone noticed that the pirates, instead of putting straight into the port, were sailing past the harbour mouth. It was probably too much to hope that they might be thinking twice about attacking Havana, but Governor Gonzalo Pérez de Angulo commanded two of his men to go and discover what de Sores was up to. They leapt into their saddles and rode off in a cloud of dust to spy on the French. Soon they galloped back, panting out the news that the ships had anchored and two boatloads of men had landed on the shore. At that very minute the invaders were approaching through the woods, bristling with extremely efficient-looking firearms, wearing helmets and breastplates and confidently brandishing French flags.

The pirates occupied Havana in half an hour. This was too much for the governor. Preserving one's honour was all very well, but waiting to be butchered was taking it to foolish extremes. He unceremoniously bundled his family and belongings together, and they retired with indecent haste to Guanabacoa on the other side of the harbour.

Commander Juan de Lobera, however, was made of sterner stuff. Keeping his head admirably in the general atmosphere of panic, he collected together sixteen people, a mixture of Spanish, Negro and Indian men, women and children, and under his direction they barricaded themselves in the little fort of the Fuerza. Commander de Lobera sent a disapproving letter to the governor, but no answer came from Guanabacoa, so he gritted his teeth and made up his mind to brave the siege. He joined his inexperienced band of defenders, and they waited with trepidation for the attack.

Spurred on by righteous indignation, excitement and the knowledge that Havana's fate rested in their hands, the occupants of the Fuerza put up an incredible fight. Even with their feeble weaponry they managed to prevent the two pirate ships from entering the harbour, and they shot down the French flag that was fluttering insolently over their city. No doubt the scene inside the Fuerza was one of chaos. It often took two people to load an harquebus, and shaking with excitement and terror as they undoubtedly were, it must have been almost impossible to pour the powder down the barrel, post in the lead ball and ram it home with a wad of rag. Every time a gun was fired with a burst of flame and a deafening report the operation would be further complicated by blinding clouds of acrid smoke. The fort rang with the combined sounds of commands, curses, choking and spluttering and the groans of the wounded.

Commander de Lobera and his companions held out bravely, but their situation became progressively worse. By 11 July only four of the harquebuses could still be fired. Several of the defenders were hurt too badly to be able to continue. Some had been killed outright.

Jacques de Sores was reluctantly impressed by the passionate defence of the Fuerza. He concluded that the furious fire from the fort could only mean that it contained something eminently worth defending. But he was reckoning without Spanish pride; having come this far Juan de Lobera was not going to give up. As the intervals between the shots from the fort lengthened, the pirates began to yell out invitations to the Habaneros to surrender. The commander would have none of it, however, and merely urged his exhausted companions to fresh endeavour. They struggled on for many hours, and the sound of the guns was punctuated by a furious exchange between the French leader and the Spanish commander.

Jacques de Sores was not a patient pirate; Juan de Lobera was extremely stubborn. It appeared that deadlock had been reached.

Darkness fell, and still the Spaniards refused to give in. Suddenly de Sores's exasperation came to a head. He was not accustomed to being kept waiting by his prospective victims, and he ordered his men to set the door of the fort alight. The dry wood caught quickly. Juan de Lobera, still undaunted, enlisted the help of a Spaniard and two black women to quench the flames, but it was no good, they were so tired and the flames leapt up so fast that they could not control them. They only just managed to escape from the blaze with their lives.

The Spaniards stood on the mound of the fort in the flickering light of the fire. De Sores demanded whether now they would be willing to give up. They were unprotected and surrounded, but de Lobera still flatly refused to surrender. The French pirate was beside himself. He began audibly to enquire whether the Spanish commander was quite insane.

This state of affairs continued throughout the night. Why de Sores did not make the most of his advantage and press forward for a quick victory is not clear; the Spanish guns could surely have been overcome without much trouble on the pirates' part. Perhaps de Sores had a sneaking admiration for the Spanish commander's bravery, so stupendous as to verge on stupidity, or perhaps he thought that the commander of the Castillo de la Real Fuerza might command a fat ransom.

Eventually dawn broke. In the light of day even de Lobera had to acknowledge the hopelessness of his position. His incredible effort had finally come to nothing. Sadly, he handed over what was left of the weaponry. The pirates rushed into the remains of the fort; now at last they would get their hands on its priceless contents. But to de Sores's incredulous disgust the only spoils to be found inside were de Lobera's comparatively meagre possessions: a few pieces of silver plate, the 2,000 pesos that made up his savings and his wife's emerald ring, all of which the pirate pocketed.

Having finally got the commander as well as the city in his clutches, de Sores was aware that he had the upper hand. He decided to open negotiations for payment of a ransom, the idea presumably being that once paid off the pirates would depart from the city and leave behind the most troublesome engagement of their career. While de Lobera was making his heroic stand in the fort, Governor Pérez de Angulo had decided that even Guanabacoa was too close to the action for comfort. He had run yet further away to the village of Bainoa, deep in the countryside. Letters began to pass back and forth between Bainoa and Havana. In an attempt to negotiate a ransom that de Sores would find satisfactory, de Lobera wrote to the governor to obtain his opinion on a suitable amount. An offer of 2,000 pesos was returned.

Jacques de Sores had a very good idea of the sort of payment that Havana could afford and refused to entertain the idea of such a paltry sum. Correspondence flew like confetti, but by now it seems that Governor Pérez de Angulo had begun to feel pricklings of shame about his undignified flight to safety. In between writing letters to the pirate he mustered an armed force of 280 men, Spaniards, Negroes and Indians, at the head of which he planned to recover both Havana and his reputation.

Pérez de Angulo led his motley band of followers to the city under cover of darkness. The plan was to enter Havana while the pirates and their prisoners slept in the citizens' houses, creep up on the building that de Sores and a few of his men had occupied and leap on them before they had time to gather their wits. Everything went beautifully as they sneaked into the slumbering city and padded softly towards the open door of de Sores's lair. Suddenly, however, the over-excited Indians could no longer contain themselves. They let out a blood-curdling war whoop, which echoed all around the town. The governor's force rushed towards the house, but the pirates had already leapt to their feet, and the door was slammed shut in Pérez de Angulo's face.

The house that de Sores had taken over was built of stone, so the governor's men didn't bother to set fire to the door. All they could think of to do was to rush around town killing every French pirate they could find. This caused de Sores to fly into a violent rage. He saw the Spaniards' actions as base, cowardly and treacherous, coming at a time when the city had been surrendered and the formal negotiating process had begun. The last straw came when he was informed that the Spanish had slain a member of his crew, who was also one of his relatives. Shaking with fury, he ordered his men to slit the throats of the captured Spaniards. The prisoners were immediately killed. Juan de Lobera's life was saved only when de Sores's companions forcibly restrained their leader from attacking him.

After this the pirates rampaged through Havana, taking everything of value that they could find. They ransacked official, religious and domestic buildings alike. Finally, they set fire to the entire city, which went up like a torch. Sheets of flame and sparks flared from the roofs, pieces of burning palm thatch filled the air, and a thick pall of smoke hung over the harbour. The pirates dressed themselves in the church vestments and caroused delightedly among the smouldering ruins until there was nothing left to drink, steal or burn. They departed on the night of 5/6 August, leaving a pitiful handful of Habaneros, grief-stricken and desolate among the cinders of their city and mourning the great numbers of dead that the pirates had left behind them.

News of de Sores's triumph in Havana travelled fast, and about a month later it reached the ears of another French pirate. The Habaneros, struggling to rebuild the city, were too broken in spirit to stop him when he arrived with his men and sacked the plantations that de Sores had not bothered with. These pirates also captured a caravel, which had unluckily just put into the harbour with a cargo of leather. They concluded their visit by burning and tearing down all the buildings that had been painstakingly reconstructed since de Sores had sailed away.

It had become clear that if the treasure flowing through Havana were to be kept safe, the Spanish crown would have to pay a great deal more attention to the city's defences. On 23 December 1555 the unhappy governor, Gonzalo Pérez de Angulo, wrote to the king asking for arms, stressing the desperate need for Havana to be fortified and begging to be replaced: 'I repeat my supplications that a governor be provided for this island; I am weary of the harvest of this earth as well as these misfortunes.'[2]

Not long afterwards both the governor's and the citizens' pleas were granted. Gonzalo Pérez de Angulo was relieved of his onerous duties and a new governor, Diego de Mazariegos, was appointed. On 21 January 1558 the Spanish King Philip II signed a decree, in which a military engineer called Bartolomé Sánchez was ordered to construct a new Castillo de la Real Fuerza to replace the one burned down by Jacques de Sores.

Bartolomé Sánchez arrived in Havana in November of the same year and began work on the fort on 1 December. It had been almost a year since the king had agreed that Havana needed the Fuerza. The long voyages between Spain and Cuba did not make for speedy communications. Once Sánchez arrived, enormous pressure was put upon him to complete the works, as every new day might bring another attack on Havana from the sea. The Spanish territories in the New World, whose treasure the new fortress was to defend, contributed 12,000 pesos to the project.

Governor de Mazariegos was impatient, hot-tempered and obsessive, a very different sort of person from his predecessor Pérez de Angulo. The one thought that occupied his mind night and day was the completion of the Fuerza. He felt that Bartolomé Sánchez was infuriatingly slow. Sánchez and de Mazariegos were soon at odds. The governor used frequently to fall into unbridled rages and stamp about among the piles of stone blocks on the building site, cursing and threatening the workers with physical violence unless they hurried up. However the fort was not completed for many years. Diego de Mazariegos had not learned one of the most important lessons for newcomers to the island: ranting at Cubans gets you nowhere. In twentieth-century Havana one sometimes sees apoplectic tourists thundering at the charming face of Cuban officialdom. This approach only results in negatives given more positively, broader and more regretful smiles, a rueful elevation of palms, eyes and shoulders and the helpful offer of another application form. In bleaker bureaucratic moments one is ready to swear that anything that gets accomplished in Cuba must be the result of a careless oversight. But in the sixteenth century the half-built state of the Fuerza could not be overlooked. It was a constant reminder of the danger that Havana was in.

Governor de Mazariegos's continual harping on the subject probably did more to hinder than to help the fort's completion. Bartolomé Sánchez had brought forty stonemasons and construction experts with him to Cuba, but he had arrived to find a completely inadequate labour force in place for the work. The governor diverted slaves from the fields, but this resulted in the crops being so severely neglected that the price of bread rocketed and visiting ships could not be adequately provisioned. Eventually all the free Negroes and mulattos in the city were ordered to abandon their trades and were put to work to build the Fuerza. Their liberty had, in effect, been revoked, as refusal to cooperate earned them a 10 peso fine or one hundred lashes.

No doubt Bartolomé Sánchez viewed the unsatisfactory state of affairs as being the fault of the governor, despite the latter's attempts to get more slaves and funds sent from Spain. Sánchez had brought the necessary craftsmen with him; he could not help it if suitable labour had not been mustered. The two men argued about design details of the fort. Then the town council took up the cry of dissatisfaction at Sánchez's performance. The houses of some of the most distinguished Habaneros had been demolished to construct the Fuerza, and so far it looked as though their homes had been needlessly destroyed.

Eventually Sánchez was dismissed. He was replaced by Francisco de Calona, who was a

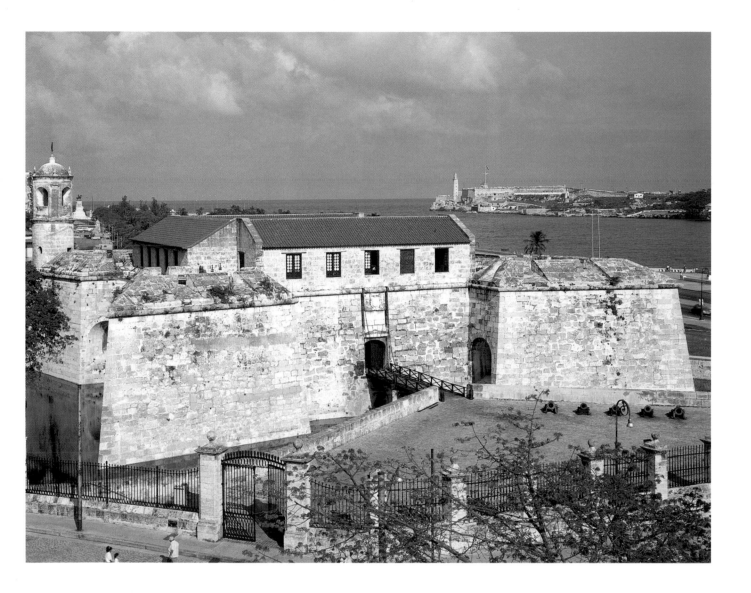

stonemason rather than an engineer, who arrived in Havana on 11 June 1562. Out of the frying pan and into the fire – the citizens were nearly driven wild by de Calona's propensity for spending his 'days and nights in play'[3] while the unsupervised building workers drifted around town and found alternative employment. The costs of the works, in marked contrast to the fort itself, were shooting up, but Francisco de Calona was retained on the job. The governor may have thought that he might be sent someone even less effective if he dismissed de Calona.

The urgency of the situation was heightened by continued pirate activity in the area. In

The Castillo de la Real Fuerza.

March 1561 a buccaneer sailed into the harbour hot on the trail of a galleon with a hold groaning with silver. Knowing the state of Havana's defences, the Spanish captain used his wits and ordered every one of the cargo of 100,000 ducados to be hurled overboard into the shallows with an expensive splash. When the pirates had beaten a disgruntled retreat all the silver was hastily scooped out again.

The Castillo de la Real Fuerza was not really finished until 1582. Even then it still lacked some final detail, and it had been a major thorn in Havana's side for over twenty years. However, when one sees it still standing today, one can only marvel that a building of such solidity and sophistication could have been built with such primitive resources. Constructed as a square with enormous triangular bulwarks at each corner, its walls are 6 metres (20 feet) thick and 10 metres (33 feet) high. Its clean lines are reflected in a moat spanned by a drawbridge leading to the fort's vaulted interior. In the courtyard in front of the fort stand cannons bearing individual names, dates and places of manufacture – 'Deceptive. Seville, 20 August 1779', 'Ardent. Barcelona, 25 September 1795'.

On the northwest corner of the fortress stands a cylindrical tower, which was built during the governorship of Juan Bitrián de Villamonte (1630–34). Surmounting the tower is a bronze statue called the Giraldilla, sculpted by Gerónimo Martín Pinzón, about which a sad tale is told. After Hernando de Soto had ordered the construction of the first Real Fuerza he sailed away from Havana on 12 May 1539 to conquer Florida. He left his wife, Doña Isabel de Bobadilla, behind as governor in his stead. Doña Isabel was 'a woman of character, and kindly disposition, of very excellent judgement and appearance'.[4] After four long years of waiting for her husband's return, the news was brought to her in Havana that he had died on the banks of the great river that he had discovered, the Mississippi. A few days later, Doña Isabel herself died of grief. The Giraldilla is said to portray her as she scans the horizon in vain for her husband's sails. In her right hand she carries a palm tree, of which only the trunk is now left, and in her left hand is the cross of Calatrava (to which order the knight Bitrián de Villamonte belonged) attached to a weathervane. Her figure is voluptuous, her hands are graceful, her hair is braided in thick ropes and her bronze robes are fluttering in the wind. The name Giraldilla is a reference to the Giralda (weathervane) tower in Seville, from where so many sailors arrived in Havana.

Above the entrance to the Fuerza are the royal arms, dating from around 1579, when the

The Castillo de la Real Fuerza: the tower and the Giraldilla.

The royal arms above the entrance to the Fuerza.

king ordered them to be carved in stone by the best craftsman to be found in Seville. Sadly, the original bell of the castle was lost; the present one was founded by Lorenzo Gerónimo del Huerto, at the order of Field Marshal Pedro Álvarez de Villarín in 1706. Bells came to be rung from the watchtowers of Havana to signal the approach of shipping, and all the citizens learned to tell by their 'language' whether the vessels were merchant or warships, how many sails they had, whether they were friends or foes, Spaniards or foreigners.

Although the second Castillo de la Real Fuerza never proved itself physically against an enemy, its mere presence was often enough to put pirates off. The governors of Cuba lived in the fortress until 1762, decorating its austere interior with statues and its exterior with ornamental balconies. Its pure angles still slice into the dark waters of its moat like the prows of galleons, and its uncompromising lines and masses sharpen against the severe slabs of shadow cast behind them by the searing tropical sunlight. At night the surface of the moat shivers with breezes from the bay and the Fuerza becomes a silvery ghost-castle, coolly shining through the gloom.

On 24 November 1585 the king sent a nervous warning to Havana, the patchy punctuation of which suggests breathless haste:

> My Governor of the Island of Cuba: Francisco Draque, it is believed in order to rob and cause whatever damage he can, has left for the Indies with several armed ships, and so that everything may be made secure and in order that you are not taken unawares and in order that you are aware of his intent in time, I have sent dispatches to all those that I wish to advise, thus after you have received this dispatch, put all those able to fight on alert and supply them with arms and whatever other items are considered necessary and fortify everything in a manner which will prevent any damage being done in order that the enemy may not do any harm.[5]

Drake's reputation had gone before the king's message to Cuba, and everyone was alert to the threat. On Thursday, 29 May 1586 the first of the dreaded sails was spotted from the Morro watchtower. As they slowly came on from the northeast the lookouts counted fourteen ships, and finally, as Martín Calvo de la Puerta wrote in June 'the entire armed fleet of Francisco Draque'[6] appeared. The Habaneros must have felt like rabbits frozen before the approach of a stoat. Their nerves were to be strung even tighter. Drake loitered outside the port for some time, neither advancing nor retreating, watching the city whose inhabitants did not dare to take their eyes off him for a moment. At one point he fired some desultory shots, which set a few of the buildings alight, but he seems in the end to have

A seventeenth-century engraving of Sir Francis Drake.

been wary of Havana's new fort. On 4 June, to everyone's intense relief, he sailed away again without attempting a landing.

This was encouraging, but the Habaneros did not want to tempt fate. In 1589–90 they began to build two more strong fortresses, one on each side of the narrow harbour mouth. The high cliff of the Morro (headland) was selected as one of the sites. It was the vantage point from which the approach of all shipping was reported and seemed an obvious choice. Its official use had dated from 30 April 1551 when the town council had ordered that a light be shown from the cliff when French vessels were seen. Two years later a small watchtower had been built there to accommodate a rota of lookouts. Ten years after that Diego de Mazariegos had a tower built on the Morro at the cost of 200 pesos.

The site of the Punta (the point) opposite the Morro was low, being on the same level as much of the city. However, it was hoped that between them the two forts, the Castillo de los Tres Santos Reyes Magos del Morro and the Castillo de San Salvador de la Punta, would

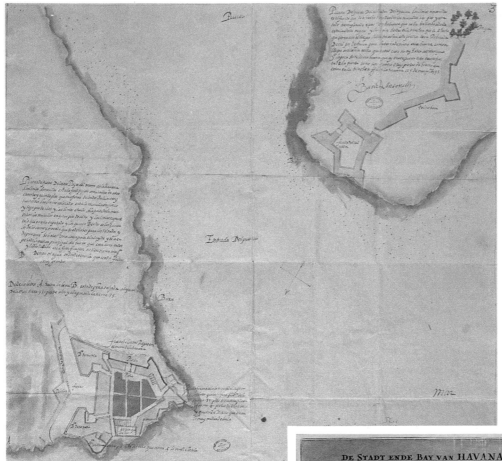

A plan of the Morro and the Punta, signed by Giovanni Baptista Antonelli on 5 March 1593.

A sixteenth-century Dutch depiction of Havana, with exaggerated landscapes and fortifications.

operate with the Fuerza in a formidable defensive triangle. The military engineer selected to construct the fortresses was Giovanni Baptista Antonelli. He was a member of an Italian family which had rendered many engineering services to the Spanish crown, and he came to Havana with his nephew Cristoforo de Roda, whom he had selected as his assistant.

There followed a repeat performance of the discord between governor and builder. Both of the forts were begun under Governor Juan de Tejeda (1589–94). He thought the construction of the Punta of greater importance than that of the Morro, saying that it had more potential for preventing landings on Havana's coastline. Antonelli, on the other hand, viewed its usefulness as minimal. He said the strategic site of the Morro was far more important. Both forts were begun under the shadow of this disagreement, which, together with the usual lack of resources, conspired to delay their completion for many years.

When Juan Maldonado Barnuevo, who was governor from 1594 to 1602, arrived in Havana, he sent a request to the king for more money. When 200,000 ducados were sent, Maldonado responded with a request for at least 200 slaves, 'for without them it is impossible to carry out these works, unless it be at double the cost'.[7]

Giovanni Baptista Antonelli, meanwhile, was suffering from a skin disease and was greatly unhappy with his present situation. He informed the king that if he were not given permission to leave Cuba he would depart without it, so in 1594 he was sent to oversee the fortifications of Panama and Cartagena.

Governor Pedro Valdés (1602–7) did much to progress the works on the Morro, overseeing the completion of the battery on which the guns called the Twelve Apostles were placed. But on 19 December 1610 Governor Gaspar Ruiz de Pereda informed the king that the fortresses of the Morro and the Punta had cost 700,000 ducados but were still incomplete. The construction of the Punta in particular was hampered by unpredictable weather. At one point almost half of it was destroyed by a storm. Given the battering that it has had over the centuries from the gigantic green waves that still crash against the sea walls of Havana, it says a great deal for the techniques of its construction that the Castillo de la Punta still stands on the edge of the harbour.

After many years of dilatoriness and disagreement, the fortifications were finally completed, and they functioned as the primary defences of the port for two centuries. The Morro towers over the mouth of the port, has a high lighthouse tower in its northwest corner and is linked to the shore 150 metres (500 feet) below by a series of ramps. It has a deep moat, cisterns, a church, officers quarters, a wine cellar, stables, dungeons and vaults, one of which is bomb-proof.

The Punta, facing it across the harbour mouth, is altogether more humble, but the combination of the two forts still presents an impressive show of military strength. Writing in 1684, the ex-pirate Exquemeling noted that:

> This is one of the renownedst and strongest places of all the West Indies… From hence is transported huge quantity of Tobacco… not onely in the leaf, but also in rowls. This city is defended by three Castles, very great and strong; two of which lie towards the Port, and the other is seated upon a hill that commandeth the Town.[8]

Pirate trouble did, however, persist into the seventeenth century. By this time the members of the profession had become highly organized, and a number of pirate captains, some ferocious, some foppish, had achieved a perverse sort of celebrity status in the Caribbean. Voyages were carefully considered. Planning meetings used to be held on deck before departure to decide on a programme of plunder. Once this had been agreed, shares of the loot were established in advance, together with the levels of compensation that would be paid out for injuries: 500 pieces of eight or six slaves for the loss of a right arm; 100 pieces of eight or one slave for an eye. Everybody took solemn oaths not to cheat each other and to abide by the ship's articles. These were eminently sensible and the penalties for dis-obedience were severe. 'That Man that shall snap his Arms, or smoak Tobacco in the Hold without a cap to his Pipe, or carry a Candle lighted without a Lanthorn,' stated the rules of the *Revenge*, Captain John Phillips's ship, 'shall receive Moses's law (that is 40 stripes lacking one) on the bare Back.'[9]

As an added defence against nocturnal attacks by aggressive intruders, a vast chain made of metal and wood could now be drawn across the harbour mouth between the Morro and Punta forts. During the day, however, it was lowered and the Habaneros had to remain on their toes, for a moment's inattention could mean the entry of an enemy into the harbour. Thomas Gage related in 1677 that when he was on board one of the fifty-two ships in the port waiting to return to Europe in convoy, two pirate ships somehow managed to sneak unnoticed into their midst. At first all the crews and passengers of the ships were cheerfully

The Castillo de los Tres Santos Reyes Magos del Morro from the Castillo de San Salvador de la Punta.

Above: The fort at the mouth of the River Chorrera.

Opposite: Remains of the city wall, with a sentry box.

preparing to leave: 'the joyfull sound of Trumpets ecchoed from ship to ship, the boats carryed welcoming messages from one to another... buen Viaje, buen Passage, was generally cryed out.' But suddenly a straggling ship was given a broadside and captured by one of the pirate vessels.

> Presently she was carried away from under our noses; the Spaniards changed their merry tunes into *voto a Dios*, and *voto a Christo*, in raging, cursing and swearing, some reviling at the Captain of the ship which was taken, and saying that he was false, and yeelded on purpose without fighting... others cursing those that took her and calling them *hijos de puta, Borrachos, infames Ladrones*, Bastards, Drunkards, infamous Theeves, and Pyrates; some taking their swords in their hands, as if they would cut them in pieces, some laying hold of their Muskets, as if they would there shoot at them, others stamping like mad men, and running about the ship, as if they would leap over bord, and make haste after them; others grinning their teeth at the poor English prisoners that were in the ship, as if they would stab them for what [they said] their Countrey-men had done.[10]

Even when the pirates were put off, it was not always by the forts. One inky night in 1655 British buccaneers landed on the coast near Havana. They crept gleefully through the woods towards the city, already visualizing their loot-laden return, but reality quickly shattered these pleasing reflections. In the velvety silence they began to hear sinister scufflings and rustlings and saw lights bobbing through the trees. An ambush! The terrified pirates took to their heels and sprinted ignominiously back to the boats as fast as their feet could carry them. Had they had the courage to investigate they would have discovered that the scuffling was made by crabs and that the lights shining in the woods were enormous Cuban fireflies.

It was well known, however, that not all the pirates of the Caribbean were this feeble. The citizens of Havana continued to strengthen the town. Small forts were built at the mouth of the River Chorrera (Santa Dorotea de Luna de la Chorrera), and at Cojímar to the east, at a cost of 20,000 ducados each. In 1674, under Captain General Don Francisco Orejón y Gastón, the construction of the city walls was begun. They took over a century to build, were 1.4 metres (5 feet) thick, 10 metres (33 feet) high, 4,892 metres (5,400 yards) long, had nine gates and were made to take 3,400 personnel. On the coastal side they ran around the edge of the bay, and on the landward side stood between the present Calles Egido, Monserrate and Zulueta. The walls were almost completely demolished in the nineteenth century, but some fragments have remained, particularly at the junction of Calle Egido and the Avenida del Puerto, and sentry boxes still stand near the northern end of Calle Cuba and in front of the Presidential Palace (between Calles Monserrate and Zulueta). Havana was divided by the construction of the wall into two areas: *intramuros*, the supposedly impenetrable area inside the walls, and *extramuros*.

Even before the walls were built, Havana's reputation as a well-fortified city had been firmly established. On 24 May 1634 a royal decree declared that it was 'the Key to the New World and Bulwark of the West Indies'.[11] The description was confirmed by the city's coat of arms bestowed on 30 November 1665: 'Azure in chief three towers [the Morro, the Fuerza and the Punta] towered fesswise Argent masoned Sable the greater towers having four merlons and the lesser having three and in base a Key [to the New World] ward to the sinister and downward Or.'[12]

'A piratical vessel, destroying a merchant ship'.

4
BUILDING FOR POSTERITY

'It is a most extensive city, of regular plan; one of the best fortified in America.... It is adorned with many public buildings, churches and convents.... In its port, one of the most vast and beautiful, the King of Spain maintains a great dockyard, an arsenal and workshops for the construction of warships.'

Villiet d'Arignon[1]

THE PEOPLE OF HAVANA HAD demonstrated their allegiance to the king by protecting his New World treasure with the fortification of their city. Now they felt able to turn their attentions to their God, and the seventeenth and eighteenth centuries witnessed a surge of pious energy. The main movers in its architectural expression were the bishops, who applied their tremendous power and influence to a brisk programme of ecclesiastical construction. Not for them the dithering and disorganization that had attended the construction of the forts. Churches sprang up swiftly all over Havana. Their interiors shone with the flames of hundreds of candles reflected in heavy gold and silver ornaments and statues of saints encrusted with jewels. The life of the city centred on these glittering monuments to religious devotion. *Placement* at mass and a strict order in processions, during which images of the saints were paraded around the city to a cacophony of bells, were jealously guarded indications of social status.

Diego Evelino de Compostela, the most celebrated of the city's builder-bishops, was born in Compostela in Coruña in 1635. His episcopate covered the turn of the seventeenth and eighteenth centuries. By the age of twenty-three he had obtained a doctorate, and prior to his arrival in Havana on 17 November 1687 he had held numerous academic offices, among them that of professor at the University of Valladolid. He was an enchanting man,

The Convento de San Francisco de Asís.

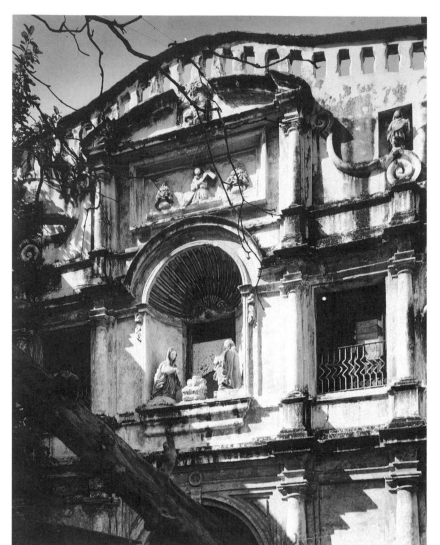

The façade of the Iglesia de Belén.

The Iglesia and Convento de Belén
by Federico Miahle.

combining true saintliness with boundless energy. He went about on foot, treated everybody with unfailing courtesy, ate only one small meal each day and preached moving sermons in a musical voice. He had several houses in Havana and donated the pleasure gardens of the one in Calle Compostela, the street to which he gave his name, as a site for a convalescent hospital. When the first nuns of Belén arrived in the city in 1704 they acquired the site for the establishment of their convent and church. The latter is the first baroque religious building in Havana. Its façade is decorated with a nativity scene set in a large niche framed with a shell, and it stands on the corner of Calles Luz and Compostela. Its construction was begun in 1712 and completed in 1718. In 1772 permission was granted to the order to erect the arch that crosses Calle Acosta to join the convent with further buildings that it had acquired. The order of Belén was housed in Calle Compostela until 1842; later the building passed to the Jesuits. The building is under restoration, and the parts that have been completed provide temporary living quarters for craftsmen who travel to Havana from all over the island to work on the restoration of the city's buildings.

Within the walls of the beautifully proportioned seventeenth-century mansion that stands on the corner of Calles Oficios and Obispo, Don Diego founded the college of San Francisco de Sales for orphan girls. The first house on the site was built by Doña Isabel Nieto, widow of Francisco Cepero, one of the conquistadors and first settlers of Cuba. She bought the land on 4 February 1559. In 1686 Diego de Compostela acquired a site adjoining the original building, and constructed the college in the form in which it is seen today. Its central patio is surrounded by galleries of stocky columns and wide, flat arches enclosing slatted doors and *mediopuntos* (semicircular fanlight windows holding stained glass in geometric or floral motifs). During the day they saturate the floors with shifting fans of blue, yellow, aquamarine, purple and red light.

Work on the convent of Santa Clara de Asís, the first nunnery to be founded in Havana, was completed by de Compostela, having been proposed early in the century by Governor General Don Pedro Valdés. The convent, which stands in the area between Calles Cuba, Habana, Sol and Luz, was intended as a refuge for girls unfortunate enough not to possess a sufficiently enticing dowry to attract suitors, on the premise that only by getting them to a nunnery could they preserve their self-respect. It is very large, having been built to house the hundreds of nuns and slaves who lived within its walls. Its interior is full of light. A restored cloister roofed with old clay tiles surrounds a large open garden overlooked by balconies. Two other cloisters, choked with rubble and littered with beautiful wooden carvings whose designs are highlighted by thick dust, await restoration. In one of them the roots of a capulí tree throttle the columns, but the fruit of the tree tastes ambrosial and looks like large golden pearls. Throughout the building the wooden ceilings are carved and re-carved with geometric designs, rippling curves and little flowers.

The interior of the Iglesia del Santo Ángel Custodio boasts a Latin inscription recording its foundation by Diego de Compostela. When he started the church in 1687 the Loma del Ángel (Hill of the Angel) on which it stands rose high above the city; now it is hidden in a forest of roofs. The church was altered in the eighteenth century. A hurricane destroyed the original tower in 1846. Finally, in the mid-nineteenth century, the exterior was reconstructed in the neo-Gothic style, but the colonial interior was left intact. José Martí, the great hero of Cuba's struggle for independence, was baptised in this church on 12 February 1853. It stands on the corner of Calles Compostela and Cuarteles, facing a small square, which was featured in Cirilo Villaverde's novel about the bewitching mulatta Cecilia Valdés.

The people of Havana adored Diego de Compostela, and when he died on 29 August 1704 a guard had to be mounted over his body to stop them taking pieces of his clothing as relics. His heart was reverently placed in a crystal vase and kept by the Order of the Barefoot Carmelites in the cloister of Santa Teresa de Jesús, which he had caused to be built, under the inscription 'his memory will live eternally as at the day of his death'.[2]

The Iglesia del Espíritu Santo on the corner of Calles Cuba and Acosta is Havana's oldest church. It was originally a hermitage dedicated in 1638 to the Holy Spirit, 'for the devotions of free Negroes'.[3] Its central nave and façade were built around 1674. In 1720 the Gothic vault of the presbytery was constructed at the behest of Bishop Gerónimo Valdés, abbot of the order of San Basilio, professor of the University of Alcalá and successor to Diego de Compostela. Gerónimo Valdés came to Cuba in April 1706, and his episcopacy lasted for twenty-three years. He completed works that de Compostela had initiated and founded the Hospital of San Lázaro and the University of Havana, which was located in the Convent of Santo Domingo.

Bishop Valdés's tremendous energy and authority stood Havana's development in good stead, but his brusqueness of manner was not universally appreciated, and sometimes his

The Convento de Santa Clara de Asís.

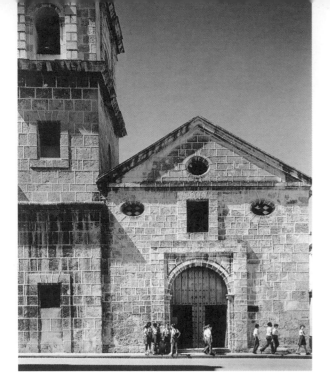

The Iglesia del Espíritu Santo.

intentions were obstructed by those whose dignity he had wounded. He died between ten and eleven o'clock on the morning of 29 March 1729 at the age of eighty-three. As he had requested, his body was buried in the Iglesia del Espíritu Santo, at eye level in a niche in a wall at the side of the choir. Over the niche was placed the following inscription:

> He who proceeded from the fire of charity rests in the ashes, to rise from the ashes. He who knew no burial, now knows the dust of the ashes, for in order that the fire should not cease, he was buried in its ashes. It is Valdés who, blowing aside the ashes of the tomb, will be reborn a new phoenix, Father of the fruitful inheritors of the globe. The most illustrious and most reverend father Don Gerónimo Valdés, of the order of San Basilio, where he received the divine light, to the dissemination of which he devoted his life, died in sanctity. He will live eternally in the homage of the Cuban people, he who attained the heights after the example of his Holy Father. He departed from our time to conquer eternity; eternal joy be unto him.[4]

The Iglesia del Espíritu Santo is a remarkable building, full of surprises. On each side of the nave is a little catacomb, one running under the choir, the other under the chapel. The one under the chapel is the more recent of the two; it was completed on 12 August 1783 by Maestro José Marín to the order of the citizens Don Juan Martín Galeano and Don Manuel Aspeitia. On the wall between the niches in the catacomb, almost erased by time and damp, is a series of paintings of the dance of death, featuring skulls crowned with tiaras and mitres. The other catacomb, underneath the choir, is the more ancient, a grim place full of bones, dust and spiders. The tree trunks with which it is roofed are still covered with bark, but the wood has the texture of bread and crumbles at a touch. The catacomb is undecorated, and dates from the same period as the nave.

If you climb up to the gallery of the church, you can turn the handle of a little carillon of twelve bells, which was placed there in the eighteenth century. At the top of the church tower hang bells made in 1709, 1732 and 1770 and the great bell of San José, which was made in 1688 and bears a crude image of the saint holding a small child by the hand.

When the Iglesia del Espíritu Santo was restored in 1958, the plaster with which the walls were covered was stripped off and unexpected details were revealed, such as the stone stars and flowers with which its Gothic vault is decorated. On the walls of the baptistery are further surprises: a carved and gilded wooden pelican in a niche and a mural painting of the top of a wrought iron gate over the existing entrance, together with a portrayal of an architectural continuation of the perspective of the church.

In the sacristy, an enormous cupboard contains an exquisite collection of baroque silver incense holders and staffs. A richly carved screen stands in front of the street door. At the end of the room is an enormous chest of drawers with tall cupboards at each end, which was ordered by Bishop Pedro Morell de Santa Cruz. It was carved in one piece from the trunk of a vast sabicú tree, and its polished curves gleam in the light reflected from the patio of the rectory, which stands next to the church.

The parish archives are preserved in the sacristy. There are volumes of 'Burials of Indians, Mulattos and Negroes', 'Baptisms of Spaniards, 1674', 'Marriages of Spaniards, from 29 July 1674' and 'Burials of Spaniards, from 1654'. Later volumes contain many famous Cuban names: Arango y Parreño, de la Luz y Caballero, Bachiller y Morales and that of Miguel de Aldama, who was baptised in the church on 26 May 1820.

The lateral nave of the Iglesia del Espíritu Santo was built by Bishop Morell de Santa Cruz around 1760. In order to complete the works, the wall containing the body of Bishop Gerónimo Valdés had to be demolished, so his remains were moved elsewhere in the church. However, scant information and the passage of time blotted the precise whereabouts of his resting-place from local memory, and for well over a century his remains were lost. On 20 April 1936, however, the Bishop was rediscovered buried under the floor of the church. His body had turned to dust, but his chasuble, cassock, stole and gloves could be clearly seen. His mitre had been placed upon his chest, with his little cross, set with seven emeralds and suspended from a silk cord. On 4 June 1961 Bishop Gerónimo Valdés's remains were placed in a final resting-place, beneath his statue, between the nave and the side aisle.

Bishop Pedro Morell de Santa Cruz held office between 1754 and 1768, and gave his name to Calle Obispo (Bishop), along which he used to take his daily constitutional. Bishop Morell de Santa Cruz continued the construction of the Iglesia del Santo Cristo del Buen Viaje (on the corner of Calles Villegas and Amargura) in the Plaza del Cristo, which had been started by Bishop Lazo de la Vega in 1732. The name of the church stems from the popularity it enjoyed during the colonial period among sailors and travellers, who used to pray in it for safe voyages.

It has a carved and painted wooden ceiling, and it is one of the oldest churches preserved in Havana. The hermitage originally constructed around 1640 on the site was built to serve as the final point of the processions of the *Via Crucis*. They left the Convent of San Francisco on Lenten Fridays and passed down Calle Amargura (Street of Bitterness). Stations of the Cross, decorated with crucifixes and altars, were set up all down the street for the occasion. The Casa de la Cruz Verde, at the junction of Calles Amargura and Mercaderes, was built during the seventeenth century. Only the external wall of the house now remains, but on its corner it still bears a stone cross, which functioned as one of the original Stations.

For many years the majestic church of San Francisco de Asís in the Plaza de San Francisco, from whose chapel the processions of the *Via Crucis* departed, was the most fashionable church in the city. From humble beginnings, it was reconstructed in 1730 in the baroque style. It boasts a principal façade detailed with statues in niches and a 40-metre (130-foot) tower, one of the highest of all the ancient religious buildings of the Americas. After it had been sullied by Protestant worship during the brief occupation of Havana by the British, it was never again used as a church, becoming instead a warehouse for military equipment. Although the chancel and dome have been destroyed, much of the enormous exterior of the building appears now as it was constructed, but nineteenth-century guide-books portray a third sacrilege: the walls of the great church plastered thickly with painted advertisements such as *Champagne de peras* (pear champagne), *Sacos para envasar azúcar* (sugar sacks) and *Chocolate Matías López, el mejor del mundo* (Matías López chocolate – the best in the world). The Convento de San Francisco de Asís, to which the church belonged, stands adjacent to it. It is composed of two large cloistered quadrangles, but it ceased to be used as a

The tomb of Bishop Gerónimo Valdés in the Iglesia del Espíritu Santo.

convent in 1841, and in 1915 the building was turned into a telephone exchange! Its restoration has recently begun.

Ringed about by its imposing castles, Havana developed during the seventeenth and eighteenth centuries from a hand-to-mouth naval station into an industrial and commercial centre in its own right. The inhabitants were becoming more prosperous. Precious woods from Cuba were in great demand in Europe for fine furniture. Large cargoes of African slaves were continually being unloaded in the port. Shipbuilding had gathered momentum; the galleons built in Havana were reputed to be the best in the Indies. The naval dockyard was established in 1723, and in it were produced stately vessels whose names conjure stirring images of stiff salt breezes and crisp bow-waves: *El Marte* (*The Mars*), *La Esperanza* (*The Hope*), *La Estrella* (*The Star*), *El Tigre* (*The Tiger*), *El Fénix* (*The Phoenix*), *El Volador* (*The Flyer*) and *El Viento* (*The Wind*).

Gone were the days of mud and palm thatch and of frantic fortification. The smuggling of tobacco and leather had become the rule rather than the exception, and nobles and merchants alike devoted both legitimate earnings and ill-gotten gains to the architectural expression of their status and new prosperity. Southern Spain, with which the city had such close links through the maritime traffic between Seville and the Indies, had long been influenced by the luxurious aesthetic traditions of the Moors. The Andalucian builders and craftsmen who began to come to Cuba in the seventeenth century brought this sophisticated language of construction with them. They translated it into a unique tropical synthesis of courtyard, column and chiaroscuro.

It is hard to guess, when walking down the narrow streets of Old Havana, at the delights which lie behind their unassuming walls. The only hints are the massive wooden doors, embellished with complicated and beautiful locks, flanked by pillars and crowned by noble escutcheons and curling baroque waves of carved stone. Stepping inside to a dark pool of polished wood, marble and mirrors one enters a world of cool sub-aquatic light and colour, a delicious relief from the blinding glare of the street. Splashes of azure, crimson, carmine, lemon and emerald-coloured light pierce the silent gloom as the sunlight glows through the panes of coloured glass in the decorative half-moon *mediopuntos* (divided with wooden struts) and *vitrales* (in which metal had replaced the wood), and long rectangular *lucetas* (panels of stained glass, in simple patterns, which run along the edges of doors and windows).

The Iglesia de San Francisco de Asís.

The colonial mansions in Havana were usually built on two main floors. The ground floor, which was devoted to commerce, was full of shops and warehouse spaces for numerous goods. The fronts of the buildings were frequently given grand covered walkways (*portales*) supported by stout Tuscan columns. The family lived on the upper floor. There, a series of cool, spacious rooms ranged around the galleries overlooked the courtyards (*patios*), light, airy, central spaces which were built in almost all the houses, large and small. In Seville, whence came their inspiration, the privilege of a patio was accorded to only the noblest mansions. These graceful open centres, which allow cooling breezes to circulate freely through the houses, were used for meetings and parties. Between the ground and first floors were entresols, in which the house slaves lived and worked and where offices were set up.

The decorative architectural features of the buildings include wide, shallow-stepped staircases enclosed in deep wells; elaborately carved window-bars (*rejas*) and banisters; slatted blinds (*persianas*), which are closed behind the *rejas* to keep out the sun, and half-doors (*mamparas*), exquisitely carved out of fine woods and set with panes of coloured and engraved glass, which serve as room dividers. The generous proportions of the graceful salons – 5–6 metres (16–20 feet) wide and 10–12 metres (33–39 feet) long – were dictated both by the large numbers of people who lived in the houses and by the frequent and lavish entertainments mounted by the inhabitants. Even some of the seventeenth-century mansions were built on the grand scale, such as that of Don Martín Calvo de la Puerta on the corner of Calles Obra Pía and Mercaderes. Some of its rooms are 16 metres (over 50 feet) long.

The Calvo de la Puertas were one of Cuba's oldest and most important families. When Don Martín's father first came to the island, he carried with him a personal letter from Philip II to the governor general, recommending that he be given an important position in keeping with his status and abilities. On 29 January 1648 Doña María de León, widow of one of the governors general, sold the house on the corner of Calles Obra Pía and Mercaderes to Martín Calvo de la Puerta for 16,000 pesos. Don Martín is remembered in Havana for the *obra pía* (pious act) which gave Calle Obra Pía its name. In 1679 he devoted the interest from 100,000 pesos to dowering five orphan girls every year. 'Rich people emulate him; poor people bless him,'[5] was the exhortation at the foot of a statue erected in his memory. Sadly, the passage of time and criminal mismanagement of the funds by Don Martín's descendants

Opposite: The Castellón escutcheon above the entrance of the Casa de la Obra Pía.
Overleaf left: The principal staircase of the Casa de la Obra Pía from the gallery.
Overleaf right: The dining room of the Casa de la Obra Pía.

reduced the number of orphans who could be dowered every year from five to one!

During its heyday the ground floor of the Casa de la Obra Pía (sometimes called Casa de Calvo de la Puerta) was full of shops, now it is full of flowers and silence. The oldest entrance to the house is in Calle Mercaderes, and the principal one is in Calle Obra Pía. The main structure of the house dates from the seventeenth century, but parts of it were remodelled in the baroque style, probably around 1793 when Don Gabriel María Cárdenas y Santa Cruz second Marqués de Cárdenas de Monte Hermosa, invested 11,863 pesos in beautifying it.

After Martín Calvo de la Puerta's death, the house passed to Nicolás Castellón y Pereira. The arms of the Castellón family, surrounded by exuberant baroque stonework, are blazoned over the main entrance in Calle Obra Pía. Some of the more geometric aspects of the carving appear almost Mayan, but it was sculpted in Spain around 1688. Later the house passed to the Cárdenas family, one of whom, Don Agustín Cárdenas y Castellón, was given the title of Marqués de Cárdenas de Monte Hermoso in recognition of services rendered during the British siege of Havana in 1762.

The entrance from the hall of the mansion into the patio is framed by curvaceous baroque mouldings, which, as they are now picked out in gleaming white against pale yellow walls, remind one irresistibly of a lemon meringue pie. The serene atmosphere of scented coolness is disrupted only occasionally, such as by the sight of a statue on the stairs of a dimpled child ferociously throttling a duck, or by the unhealthy state of obesity of the other sculpted cherubs, which pop up disconcertingly in unexpected places all over the house.

Another fascinating house, which passed from hand to hand over the years, is Calle Tacón number 12, which now functions as the Archaeological Department of the Office of the City Historian. The building was first mentioned in a document dated 21 April 1644, when Doña María Díaz de Rivadeneyra Sotomayor gave it to her daughter Doña Luisa de Carvajal, who passed it in turn to *her* daughter, Doña Lorenza de Carvajal, in a will dated 6 August 1659. Doña Lorenza did not, however, continue the tradition by bequeathing the house to her own daughter. There is some speculation that the unfortunate girl, whose name is not recorded, brought disgrace upon the family by becoming pregnant. She was sent to the Convent of Santa Clara, although her mother appears to have been quite wealthy enough to provide her with a dowry.

Even under these circumstances, Doña Lorenza's choice of beneficiary for the house is a

Mural under restoration at Calle Tacón number 12.

surprise. In 1700 the building was inherited by Juana de Carvajal, a mulatta to whom Doña Lorenza had given her liberty on 1 February 1698 on the condition that she remained with her mistress until the latter's death. Juana de Carvajal set about improving and embellishing her property, building an upper floor in around 1725 to what had until then been only a single-storey house.

When Juana died in 1733 her niece inherited the building, and on 5 November 1748 she sold it to Doctor Don Pedro José Calvo de la Puerta (nephew of Don Martín Calvo de la Puerta), who also bought the house next door, Calle Tacón number 8. Don Pedro was Mayor of Havana in 1762 when the British attacked the city, and he displayed such bravery during the siege that he was given the title of Conde de Buena Vista. Don Pedro died on 13 October 1781, but it was during his period of ownership that the most exciting feature of the house was created. Between 1763 and 1767 one of the rooms in what had been Calle Tacón number 8 was decorated with a series of beautiful and eccentric murals. Some believe that they were ordered by Don Pedro's son, Don Nicolás Calvo de la Puerta, a professor at Havana University who was to inherit the property and install in it the first chemistry laboratory in the city.

The paintings, which were revealed only after twenty-six other layers of mural painting and whitewash had been removed, are being restored, but it is already easy to enjoy them. One panel depicts a pleasure garden, with formal lawns, a fountain spouting three powerful jets of water and a trellis covered with red roses in full bloom. Multicoloured birds swoop among the branches of the trees, against a pink, blue and violet sky. Gentlemen in tricorne hats with their hair in queues bow to ladies in voluminous silks. Elaborate carriages are drawn past picturesque ruins by fat, high-stepping horses. Another scene shows a bridge, spanning a lake upon which someone is sailing in a small boat. In the distance, the spires and towers and domes of a large city can be seen. Beside the lake a lady in red is playing a recorder, accompanied on the violin by an admirer, while two other ladies dressed in blue and yellow look on; one is languidly fanning herself. Further panels show galleons sailing towards palm-fringed shores and troops of soldiers marching along a road, while in another, in an ornamental park, gentlemen are attended by their black grooms, priests are having earnest discussions among the topiary and ladies chat as they saunter along the paths.

As well as attending mass, tricked out in all their finery and assessing everyone else's, and

The Casa de Don Mateo Pedroso.

going to parties, the citizens of eighteenth-century Havana enjoyed a wide variety of public entertainments. Among them were the fiestas, which featured the *juego de cañas* (jousting with sticks of cane). Bullfights were tremendously popular; no fewer than twenty-four of them were organized to celebrate the birth of a royal prince in 1605. Gambling remained an obsession, and after royal efforts to ban it came to nought official gaming establishments were opened in the city.

A house that was to remain at the brilliant centre of Havana's social life until the mid-nineteenth century was the Casa de Don Mateo Pedroso, which stands on Calle Cuba near its junction with Calle Cuarteles, facing the bay. It was built around 1780 by Don Mateo Pedroso y Florencia, the mayor of Havana and a member of one of the oldest and most influential families in Cuba. A description of the great size of the building was given by the 'Cuban Scheherazade'[6] Doña Mercedes de Santa Cruz, Condesa de Merlín, when she came back to Havana from France in 1840. One can well understand the beautiful Condesa's delighted remark at returning to Cuba, 'I love you and I don't know why',[7] when one sees this enormous mansion in which she held court, showing off her Parisian refinements, and was waited upon by a hundred slaves. The family used to dine on the wide upper gallery, taking advantage of the evening breeze from the patio, and the house still has a tremendous feeling of luxury and a pronounced air of the Arabian Nights, with its foliate door arches and profusion of patterned tiles. Now there are craft shops in the entresol, and by the patio there are a bookshop and a bar. There can be no more soothing way to pass a day than to spend it in the quiet of the Casa Pedroso, soaking up poetry and rum.

Havana's economy continued to grow, swelled by greater agricultural activity, and cotton and coffee were added to its exports. Sophisticated methods of tobacco cultivation were introduced by Canary Islanders arriving in Cuba. Europe echoed with satisfied sneezes induced by Cuban snuff pinched from jewelled boxes. Staggering profits were also being made in the slave trade. The Casa de la Condesa de la Reunión de Cuba, a house embellished with coloured tiles and curvaceous balconies which stands in Calle Empedrado between Calles Cuba and San Ignacio, was acquired from the Garro family by Santiago de la

María de las Mercedes de Santa Cruz y Montalvo, Condesa de Merlín.

Cuesta y Manzanal, Conde de la Reunión de Cuba and one of the island's first slave traffickers.

The development of the city increased in proportion to its growing wealth. The first public lighting was introduced in 1768, and on 24 October 1790 the city's first newspaper was printed. Havana progressed from its austere seventeenth-century beginnings to a sumptuous synthesis of the baroque, the Moorish and the Gothic: 'a warehouse for columns, a jungle of columns, columns to infinity.'[8] It was full of houses embellished with fine marble floors, ever more intricately carved ceilings and brightly coloured murals, paintings, tapestries, sparkling chandeliers, luxurious draperies and massively ornate furniture.

Ever-increasing numbers of ships calling at Havana during the seventeenth century caused the city to develop rapidly.

77

5

CITY SQUARES, THE NOBILITY AND THEIR PALACES

'Early one morning she went to the market in the Plaza Vieja... rising from the centre was a stone fountain composed of a wide bowl and four dolphins from which gushed intermittent streams of thick, muddy liquid which Negro water vendors eagerly collected in barrels to be sold throughout the city for half a silver real each. From this central point paths... were defined by the stalls laid out on the ground by the traders without any apparent order or classification. One would be for vegetables, another for live poultry, or fruits, or game, or edible roots, or caged birds, or river and sea fish still in the fishermen's baskets, or freshly killed meat hung by its head in barrels or from hooks; everything breathed humidity... fruit rinds and green maize husks, feathers and mud, without any covering or awning. There was not a decent face to be seen among the peasants and Negroes, some poorly dressed, others almost naked... and above were the blue heavens... in which the odd cloud appeared like the transparent, gauzy wing of an invisible angel.'

Cirilo Villaverde[1]

HAVANA'S PAST is concentrated in its squares into an essence so rich that it is indigestible unless taken in small sips. Each plaza has a distinctive character, but they all ring with the echoes of processions, fiestas, contests, markets, proclamations, flirtations and fights. There is always a new discovery to be made in the squares and familiarity breeds a desire for further familiarity. Their character changes with the light. They are brisk and sharp on sunny blue and white mornings; ancient and tragic when veils of rain stream from the balconies; voluptuous when a hot midnight is illuminated by lamps and vibrates with guitar music and the muffled heartbeat of an African drum.

In its early days most of Havana's extravagant fiestas used to be held in the squares. In 1760, after the proclamation of Carlos III as king, the celebrations continued for five months! They began with a solemn mounted parade of government officials and troops in the Plaza de Armas, where a large model of the Castillo de los Tres Reyes del Morro was erected. From early in the morning the citizens had been decorating the balcony of the town council building with damask hangings and magnificent portraits of the king and queen, with a golden image of the coat of arms of Havana at their feet. Models of the Castillos de la Punta and de la Real Fuerza were placed in the

The Plaza de Armas:
the Palacio de los Capitanes Generales
from the Palacio del Segundo Cabo.

centres of the Plazas Belén and Vieja respectively. The officials, dressed in cloaks and hats of crimson velvet, processed from square to square to the accompaniment of cannon shots and ringing bells, formally honouring the new king with declamations over the models of each of the three castles symbolized on Havana's coat of arms. They collected the royal standard from the house of Don Gonzalo Recio de Oquendo, official organizer of the royal fiestas, which was located in the Plaza de Armas; its interior was hung with crimson damask and shone with the lights of countless white wax candles reflecting off ornate silver holders. The flag was taken to the Plaza Vieja where everyone dismounted, the proclamation was read out, and the royal standard was lifted and waved back and forth while the people shouted 'Viva! Viva! Viva!'

The Plaza de Armas is at the seaward end of Calles O'Reilly and Obispo, and it is the oldest square in Havana, redolent of enormous political power, military might and the gracious formalities of the evening promenade for which it became the celebrated setting in the nineteenth century. In the centre of its verdant garden stands a statue to Carlos Manuel de Céspedes, hero of the Ten Years' War. Around the garden are marble seats upon which Cubans lounge and chat in the shade.

Facing the garden stands the tremendous Palacio de los Capitanes Generales, from where the iron hand of the governors enforced Spanish domination over the entire island, and particularly over the city of Havana. In its exterior arcade stands a statue which was replaced by the portrayal of de Céspedes in the centre of the square; it is of Fernando VII and was erected in 1834. Viewed from the front it is a noble representation of the Spanish king in all his majesty, robed and ruffed, holding his plumed hat in one hand and a scroll of parchment in the other. But when visitors to Havana catch a glimpse of Fernando from the side there is no getting away from the fact that the jauntily-angled parchment roll in his hand assumes an alternative identity... the air shakes with stifled giggles.

Uppermost in the minds of Havana's first settlers was the need to establish a nucleus around which their town could be constructed, and they chose a site in the area of the present Castillo de la Real Fuerza. Initially only primitive buildings were erected there; although the parish church built on the west side of the square in 1555 was made of stone and tiles, it too was a very simple affair. The site functioned for some time as the focal point of the settlement, but after the Real Fuerza was completed it was requisitioned for military

80

Above left: Fernando VII ignoring visitors' sniggers.

Above right: Governor General Felipe de Fondesviela, Marqués de la Torre.

Below: The Plaza de Armas in the nineteenth century.

exercises. However, when two grand governmental edifices were built there during the second half of the eighteenth century it once more became the centre of administrative and recreational life in the city.

Four important buildings face into its generous central area. The Palacio del Segundo Cabo (the Palace of the Second Lieutenant) next to the Real Fuerza is first documented in the records of a meeting of the town council on 20 December 1770, when the governor announced that he had received royal orders to build a post office. Its construction, supervised by the Cuban engineer Antonio Fernández Trevejos y Zaldivar, was completed around 1773. The style of the building, while retaining the atmosphere of the Cuban baroque, has a formality and order with a flavour of neoclassicism. This restraint became architecturally significant when in the same year Governor General Felipe de Fondesviela, Marqués de la Torre, took the appearance of the palace as a model for that of the neighbouring Palacio de los Capitanes Generales. After fulfilling its role as a post office, which was moved to the Palacio de los Marqueses de Arcos in the Plaza de la Catedral, the building was used successively as the office of the royal estate (with the counting houses and treasury being located on the ground floor, the secretary's office and archives in the entresol and the superintendent's offices on the first floor) and the court of justice. Finally, in 1854 it became the residence of the second lieutenant, who served as vice-governor general.

The governor general himself resided in splendour next door in the glorious palace that still dominates the square. It also housed the offices of the town council, which were located in the Plaza de San Francisco until, on 15 October 1768, Hurricane Santa Teresa damaged them beyond repair. On 28 January 1773, after the customary period of civic indecision, the Marqués de la Torre presented a proposal to the council in which the church in the Plaza de Armas would be knocked down, the square would be redefined and the Palacio de los Capitanes Generales would be built 'in imitation of the Royal Post Office which has been magnificently constructed on the north side.'[2]

It took until 1776 for his plan for the 'capacious and magnificent Plaza de Armas with buildings appropriate to the grandeur of this city to be begun with the construction of the Palacio de los Capitanes Generales. The building materials for the palace were in keeping with the grandiose ambition of de la Torre's plan – 100,000 bricks from Málaga, beautiful wrought and cast iron *rejas* from Bilbao and marble from Genoa – but its construction was a

The patio of the Palacio del Segundo Cabo.

painful process initiated by ten badly paid slaves. A few years later, only three of them were left alive. Governor Luís de las Casas, the first to occupy the palace, was finally able to move in on 23 December 1791. The ground floor housed various government departments, coach houses, stables, guardrooms and a prison, and the governor occupied the salons on the upper floor. The street below his windows was and still is surfaced with wooden cobbles. It would not have done to disturb the great man's siesta with the clatter of carriage wheels on stone.

There is no frivolity about the courtyard of the palace. It is grand and stately, with no-nonsense arches, and tall palms echo the majestic lines of its columns. This was the public space built for orders and reprimands, efficiency and influence. But high in the towering stairwell a round stained glass window splashes its colours against the opposite wall, and at the top of the great flight of marble stairs trodden by sixty-five governors general are their own luxurious quarters. High ceilinged and gracious, they are as crammed today as they were then with rich furnishings and countless works of art, for the palace is now the Museum of the City of Havana. There are glimpses of two enormous marble baths in the shape of nautilus shells, gilded mirrors, gleams of light cast from vast chandeliers onto the polished floors and in a corner a spotted marble veil blows across the laughing marble face of a young girl. Here the cream of Havana society disported itself above the bones of those who were buried there when their church stood on the site.

On a plaque now mounted inside the palace is a *memento mori*: 'Accidentally injured by a weapon, Doña María de Cepero died here in 1557. Padre Nuestro, Ave María.'[3] Doña María was killed during the ritual firing of harquebuses at a feast that she had organized.

The Museum of the City is crammed with treasures and curiosities. Silver spurs; canes with handles made of tiger's eye, gold and ivory; duelling pistols in a green silk-lined case; flower arrangements made of shells, which tremble delicately at the slightest vibration; the governor's porcelain plates; cockerel spurs in a decorative box; erotic prints of Mars and Venus, Bacchus and Ariadne and Cupid and Psyche, all toying vigorously with one another; a nineteenth-century fire engine, with gleaming brass fittings, made by Shand Mason & Co, Engineers, London; a picture of ferns and fluttering ribbons made from the hair of one María de Jesús Sedano de Perdomo as a *recuerdo* (keepsake) for her children.

In a corner of the ground floor gallery is a flight of steep stone steps leading to the network of dungeons beneath the palace where dark passages, barely shoulder width, snake back and

The throne room of the Palacio
de los Capitanes Generales.

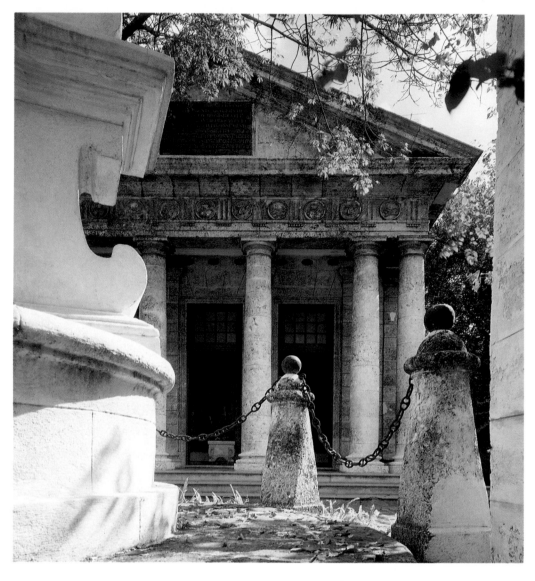

The Templete.

forth and suddenly open out into vaulted chambers. In the courtyard of the palace there is a
peacock which rustles around in the bushes and resolutely refuses to display his colours. For
a while he disappeared completely, and it was thought that perhaps the ghoulish echoes of
peacock shrieks had become too much even for the enthusiasm of the City Historian, who
darts about his mysterious office in the palace like Prospero, surrounded by books, relics and
symbols, brewing elaborate plans for the restoration of Havana to its former glory and
occasionally emerging to fascinate audiences with strange and wonderful stories. Now the
peacock has reappeared. Luckily for all concerned he has lost his voice and found a mate.

In the entresol of the palace is a collection of gravestones from the old Cementerio de Espada, interspersed with beautiful wreaths of white porcelain roses and jasmine and cut-glass lamps from funeral carriages. One poignant pair of gravestones records the deaths of two boys: Aurelio Luís Plá y Silva, who died of cholera on 20 March 1866, and his brother Justo Joaquín, who followed him on 10 May. Another gravestone honours Teresa Garro y Risel, Countess of Fernandina, whose portrait hangs in Havana's Palacio de Bellas Artes, while alongside it is that of her husband, José María de Herrera y Herrera, Count of Fernandina, Grandee of Spain, who died on 19 February 1864.

Facing the Palacio de los Capitanes Generales from the opposite side of the square is the Palacio del Conde de Santovenia. It belonged initially to the Condesa de San Juan de Jaruco, but was bought at the beginning of the nineteenth century by the Conde de Santovenia, whose initials are incorporated into its decorative iron balcony rail. He held sumptuous parties in his apartments upstairs, while downstairs a dreadful reek of oil and fish drifted out over the Plaza de Armas from his warehouses.

By the end of the century the palace had been scrubbed down and turned into the Hotel Santa Isabel. Run by one Colonel Lay from New Orleans, it was considered to be one of Havana's better hostelries, even by the standards of the more vociferously critical of the city's visitors.

On the same side of the square by a ceiba (silk-cotton) tree stands the Templete, a neoclassical temple built in the first half of the nineteenth century on the spot where the first mass and town council meeting were held in Havana in 1519. Its tiny interior is dominated by three large paintings by Jean Baptiste Vermay, who was brought to Cuba by Bishop Juan José Díaz de Espada y Fernández de Landa to continue the frescoes begun in the cathedral by Giuseppe Perovani. Vermay, born on 15 October 1786, was a follower of Jacques Louis David, had studied in both Rome and Florence and went on to found an art school in Havana.

The works in the Templete are representations of the first mass, the town council meeting and the inauguration of the Templete itself on 19 March 1828, in which many contemporary personalities of Havana are portrayed. In the centre of the picture is the Captain General Dionisio Vives and his black page Tonda, who later became a captain in the army. On the right-hand side is Bishop Espada, and in the bottom right-hand corner is his protégé, the painter himself. In the far left-hand corner is the painter's wife, with her black slave. There is a crowd milling about behind the railings. One of the pretty ladies kneeling in the foreground seems to be finding the speeches tiring. Tapping her hand with her fan she looks dismally out from the canvas. Perhaps she had pins and needles. That was nothing to what poor Vermay suffered in Havana. While painting in the cathedral he fell from a great height onto the marble floor, cutting his hands and feet, dislocating his shoulders and breaking his nose. In 1833 a cholera epidemic, in which almost 8,000 people died in the space of three months, killed both the dedicated artist and his wife. Now their remains are kept in an urn in front of the paintings in the Templete. His memory was commemorated by his friends with the words:

> Here lies Vermay. The pure light
> Of enthusiasm illuminated his mind;
> His soul was honest and ardent,
> He had the tender heart of the artist.
> He was a painter who sowed in our land
> The powerful seed of his art,
> And in every gentle and generous heart
> Left profound love, distress and sorrow.[4]

The second of Havana's squares, the Plaza Vieja (old square), between Calles Teniente Rey, Muralla, San Ignacio and Inquisidor, was originally known as the Plaza Nueva (new square). It was begun around 1584 by popular demand after Diego Fernández de Quiñones, the commander of the Castillo de la Real Fuerza, irritatingly decided that he required the Plaza de Armas for military drills. The Plaza Vieja was residential. It had no churches or domineering government buildings. As it was reasonably near the port with its busy wharves, many of the wealthy members of the first society of ship owners made their homes there. From their ornate balconies they used to watch royal proclamations, official processions, masked balls, bullfights, fireworks and executions. Competitions on horseback were also held. These included the *juego de cañas* (game of canes), the *juego de sortija*, in which rings suspended at a certain height had to be threaded onto a short stick by the rider of a galloping horse, and the *juego de alcancías*. In this contest the riders would break open clay moneyboxes filled with flowers, scented powders, coloured water and ribbons as they thundered past in a cloud of dust.

The Plaza Vieja was alternately used as a huge public salon and a commercial centre. Markets were held there in which meat, vegetables and fruits (pineapples, bananas and the delectable *mamey colorado*, 'angels' sweetmeats') were sold by peasants and free Negroes. The ground floors of the surrounding buildings were set up as independent shops with their own entrances.

The noise in the square when the market was in full swing must have been incredible. A French traveller to Cuba in the early nineteenth century found the smells and sights staggering, too.

> I used to go to the Plaza Vieja. There, ghastly things and a dreadful smell awaited me … the *tasajo* [dried meat], the bacon, the beef and pork, half dried, half salted, half rotten and most disagreeable to see and touch. Old black women, sellers of eggs or meat, surprised me by their excessive fatness. … They were dressed in the manner of colonial women of olden times, in a simple skirt and a shirt gathered in pleats at the shoulder. … M. Bernardin de Saint Pierre … says that a coconut, stripped of its fibre, has an identical appearance with its three holes, to the anterior and posterior parts of a Negress … If he could have seen the round, fat shoulders of the Negresses in the Plaza Vieja, with what would he have compared them?[5]

The square has suffered over the centuries, and although it is being restored with enormous care the process is slow. Many of its scarred and crumbling palaces, propped up by scaffolding, scribbled with electrical wiring and powdered with fine white dust, present a sad picture. The worst horror perpetrated there was the construction of an unspeakably hideous car park in the centre of the square, during the years of this century when revenue rather than restoration was the priority uppermost in the authorities' minds.

Much has been done to erase the evidence of the offending edifice from the square, but the exquisites of Old Havana must be writhing in their graves at the havoc that neglect has wreaked on their beautiful homes. They were always particular about the Plaza Vieja. When, in 1835, Governor Tacón built a formal market in front of the houses, a howl of protest arose from the aristocratic residents who had thereby been deprived of their light and air, but their complaints fell on deaf ears. Although the Mercado de Cristina was demolished in 1908, its construction marked the advent of a gradual process of destruction and alteration whose effects are only now being painstakingly reversed.

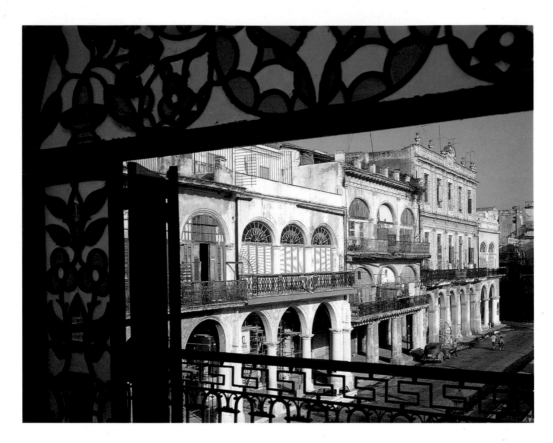

One of the mansions to rise like a phoenix from builders' rubble is the Casa de los Condes de Jaruco (Calle Muralla numbers 107–111 between Calles Inquisidor and San Ignacio). At the end of the eighteenth century the mansion was owned by Don Gabriel Beltrán de Santa Cruz y Aranda, who received the title of Conde de San Juan de Jaruco in 1770. He built the slender-columned gallery and balcony which front the seventeeth-century building. His title later passed to his nephew, Don Joaquín de Santa Cruz y Cárdenas.

Don Joaquín was born in Havana on 10 September 1769, and both his parents died when he was very young. However, he went on to a shining military career, and the house in Calle Muralla became a centre for Havana socialites and visiting foreign dignitaries. It was also the childhood home of María de las Mercedes de Santa Cruz y Montalvo, his daughter, who was to achieve fame and fortune as the Condesa de Merlín.

After the intimidatingly cavernous entrance hall, the heart of the house is compact and friendly. Its broad staircase rises past the entresol and a window in the stairwell, barred with carved eighteenth-century *rejas* and overlooking the courtyard, to a spacious upper gallery. The building now houses the organization responsible for the sale of the work of Cuban

Above: Houses in the Plaza Vieja,
seen from the Casa de los Condes de Jaruco.

Opposite: The Casa de los Condes de Jaruco.

artists. People stride in and out of the offices with armfuls of drawings and lean on the sun-blistered balcony rail to yell down at friends disappearing into the dark doorways below. Others sit in white wicker rocking chairs dreamily watching the house martins that nest under the eaves. The walls of the house are painted with bands of whimsical murals: lyres, flowers, fruit and flourishes in blue, ochre, terracotta, green and gold. At night pattern is piled upon pattern as the undulating shadows of the *rejas* are cast across the murals by the bright lights shining on poetic, comic or musical events in the courtyard below. Behind the outer balcony on the upper floor are three flamboyant nineteenth-century *mediopuntos* of floral and geometric design. The arms of the Jarucos stand proudly over the heavy door to the mansion. On it there is a large lock in the form of an African girl with a strange ridge across her cheeks, perhaps this is tribal scarring, or perhaps it represents an actual instrument of torture fitted to recalcitrant slaves.

In addition to the future Condesa de Merlín, several other celebrated women lived in the Plaza Vieja. The modest house on the corner of Calles San Ignacio and Teniente Rey belonged to the famous sisters Doña María Loreto and Doña María Ignacia Cárdenas y Santa Cruz, known throughout Havana as 'las beatas Cárdenas'. The house had previously been owned by a possessor of irresistible charms called Doña Luisa de Estrada. She married twice; her first husband Francisco Cepero died and left her a fortune; the second, Pedro Valdés, was a governor general. She departed this world leaving large sums of money, several houses, a cattle ranch, quantities of jewels, among them a golden lizard set with emeralds, and forty slaves. Doña Luisa Peñalver y Navarrete, Marquesa de Casa Calvo, lived on the same side of the square at Calle San Ignacio number 364. Even by the high Havana standards she too was considered sublimely lovely, and when she died on 26 March 1792 one besotted gentleman wrote sorrowfully that the city had lost its most exalted deity.

Opening out from the corner of Calles San Ignacio and Empedrado is the Plaza de la Catedral, which was declared by Walter Gropius to be the finest colonial square in America and was the last to be built within the city walls. Originally one of the less salubrious areas of Havana, lying at a low point into which all the local rainwater drained, it was known during the seventeenth and much of the eighteenth centuries as the Plazuela de la Ciénaga, the Little Square of the Swamp. One good downpour can still render it pretty damp, and a photograph taken in 1880, mildly entitled 'A Rainy Day in the Plaza de la Catedral', shows a positively Venetian scene of columns rising out of a sheet of water.

In 1577 the inhabitants of the area, tired of sloshing about in the marsh which was hampering the town's development, each contributed 300 reales and the labour of their own slaves for the construction of a wooden bridge, which ran along the site and later became Calle San Ignacio. About ten years afterwards, in response to the needs of both the people of Havana and the ships which were putting into the port in increasing numbers, a cistern was built in the square. Five years later a branch of the Zanja Real, an irrigation channel which carried the water of the River Almendares to the city, was sited there. The bridge caused the area to be considered as an integral part of the settlement with potential for development. However, the people of Havana were keen to retain open spaces within the city that could be used as public squares. On 20 December 1632 the crown complied with their wishes by decreeing that the site of the Plaza de la Catedral need not be sold off for construction. During the early seventeenth century it functioned as a market and meeting-place for Havana fishermen, and primitive buildings began to be erected around its perimeters. Its present appearance dates from the eighteenth century.

The Palacio del Conde de Casa Lombillo (Calle Empedrado 151 between Calles Mercaderes and San Ignacio) was built during the first half of the eighteenth century for Don José Pedroso y Florencia. Whoever named the house was misinformed, for the Conde de Casa Lombillo never lived there. It was inherited in 1871 by Doña Concepción Montalvo y Pedroso, who was married to Don José Lombillo y Herce, a Havana slave trader. The title of Conde de Casa Lombillo belonged not to Don José but to his brother Gabriel.

On occasions nowadays, when fashion shows are held in the square, the palace is used as a dressing-room. Crowds of beautiful half-naked mulatta girls run in and out of the rooms, squealing agitatedly about missing shoes, scarves and earrings. Before they dance from between the columns into the bat-filled glare of the spotlights they pause in the entrance, twitching at each other's dresses, and the darkened hall hisses with frantic last-minute whispers. As they leap forth with unseeing smiles, appreciative masculine stares focus from the shadows of the gallery fronting the Palacio de los Marqueses de Arcos next door. This house, at Calle Mercaderes number 16 between Calles Empedrado and O'Reilly, was built in the 1740s for the royal treasurer, Diego Peñalver de Angulo y Calvo de la Puerta.

His son Ignacio Peñalver y Cárdenas, who occupied the same official position as his

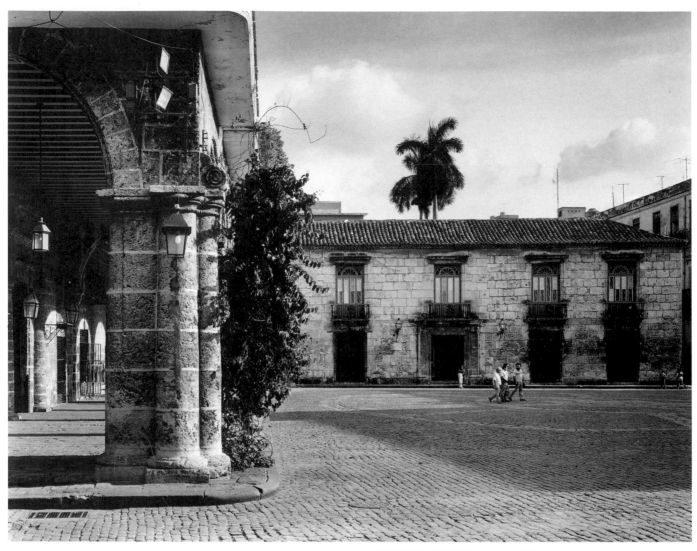

The Plaza de la Catedral.

A sixteenth-century plaque
commemorating the Zanja Real.

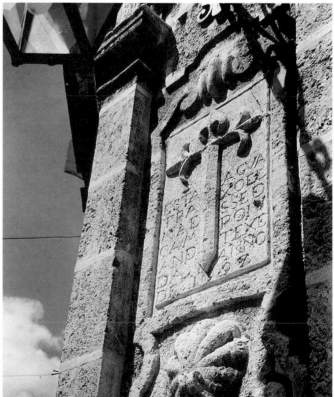

father, inherited and improved it so that it could function both as his residence and as the treasury. In 1792, Ignacio Peñalver received the title of Marqués de Arcos, but during the first half of the nineteenth century the family moved away from the palace. It became a post office, and officials scurried up and down the wide stairs previously swept by the silks of the Arcoses. Now a most unpleasant mailbox leers from its wall, a grotesque face which looks as though it might spit your correspondence back at you if it has not already had your fingers when you posted the letters.

The palace facing the cathedral was built for Governor General Don Luis Chacón around 1720. It looks much simpler and more ancient than the other houses in the square, for it has been altered very little since its construction. In 1769 the Chacón family sold the house to Don Miguel Calvo de la Puerta. After his death his widow Doña Felicia de Herrera left it. Following a succession of owners it eventually came into the possession of Don Francisco Marty y Torrens.

Pancho Marty was an ex-smuggler who, although supposedly reformed, went on to apply the cut-throat entrepreneurial skills of his previous trade to making an enormous fortune, first out of fish and later in theatricals. During the nineteenth century the house served as offices, first for notaries and later for a newspaper. In the 1930s it was turned into the headquarters and bar of a rum manufacturer. Now it houses the Museum of Colonial Art and is stuffed to the eaves with stained glass, carved wood, elaborate locks and doorknockers, delicate wrought iron, lamps, stirrups, harnesses, carriages, Baccarat crystal, silver, porcelain, marble, marquetry and a piano inscribed 'William Stoddart, Maker to their Majesties and the Royal Family, Golden Square, London'. In one of the bedrooms stands the entire set of gleaming caoba-wood bedroom furniture that belonged to the Condes de Jaruco who lived in the Plaza Vieja.

On the west side of the square, craftworks are sold from the gallery on the ground floor of a twentieth-century building built in the colonial style on the site of a nineteenth-century bath-house. It is retiring and inoffensive and does not presume to compete; a perfect place in which to spend sweltering Cuban afternoons gazing out over the evocative stones of the square. It is built onto the Palacio de los Marqueses de Aguas Claras. The site of this small palace, owned during the sixteenth century by Governor General Gonzalo Pérez de Angulo, was bought in the 1760s and built upon by Don Sebastián Peñalver de Angulo. His brother Diego lived on the other side of the square in the Palacio de los Marqueses de Arcos. Don Sebastián fell into bad odour in Havana when he was accused of collaboration with the British during their occupation of the city, so no doubt the father's defects were graciously overlooked when his son Gabriel was awarded the title of Conde de Casa Loreto. After Don Sebastián's death the house was sold to Don Antonio José Ponce de León y Maroto, the first Marqués de Aguas Claras. Now the fountain in the courtyard is the centrepiece of a restaurant called El Patio. In the somnolent pause between the waitress taking one's order and shuffling back with the wrong drink, one can climb the stairs and flop into a furry old velvet chair in the entresol or peer from the rather rickety balconies at the pattern of cobbles in the square below.

Havana's cathedral, the Catedral de la Virgen María de la Concepción Inmaculada, although it is not itself large, dwarfs the pretty little palaces around the square. It is not beautiful but extravagant, and it exercises a peculiar spell, which has much to do with disbelief. Its eccentric towers are of different heights, widths and designs but they seem symmetrical. At dusk it is open-armed, at noon forbiddingly stony. Mad waves of baroque break about its severe pillars. It has been described as one of the most beautiful façades in Latin America, 'music turned to stone'[6] and 'huge but not fine, old yet not ancient, dilapidated and, as it were, worm eaten',[7] and it has always been an architectural magnet towards which everyone, loving it or loathing it, has been drawn. The cathedral was begun in 1748 by the Jesuits, but it was still unfinished when the order was expelled from Cuba by Carlos III in 1767. In 1772 the works were resumed, and the building was finally completed around 1777. A royal decree of December 1793 confirmed its elevation from parish church to cathedral with the declaration that 'the beautifully carved stones of a church of this consequence... are clamouring from their walls for the distinction of [the title of] cathedral'.[8]

Next to the cathedral is the Seminario de San Carlos y San Ambrosio, a very large building, the façade of which faces the bay, built on three floors surrounding a generous central patio in which there is a remarkable atmosphere of serenity and a silence so profound that you can hear a leaf spring up as a lizard jumps off it. The history of the seminary began with an establishment founded by Bishop Juan de las Cabezas Altamirane in 1605, and in 1721 the Jesuits established a college on the present site and maintained it until their expulsion from Cuba. The Real Colegio y Seminario de San Carlos y San Ambrosio opened its doors

Opposite: The Catedral de la Virgen María de la Concepción Inmaculada.

Overleaf left: The Seminario de San Carlos y San Ambrosio at dawn.

Overleaf right: A staircase and *rejas* at the Seminario de San Carlos y San Ambrosio.

on 3 October 1774, and young men wishing to follow an ecclesiastical career have studied there ever since. It is a venerable building with a particularly impressive staircase. Its steps have been worn into ripples like sand dunes, and its massive caoba-wood banister looks all the more beautiful for having its carvings outlined by a fine powdering of white dust. The patio of the seminary is full of trees and flowers: yagruma, frangipani, ginger lily and many different palms, ferns and creepers.

For just over a century a casket containing what the Spanish believed to be the ashes of Christopher Columbus was kept in the cathedral, before it was returned to Spain in 1899. The remains had been brought to Havana from Santo Domingo after Hispaniola (Haiti and the Dominican Republic) passed to France in 1795. It is now thought that the ashes were those of Columbus' son Diego, but none of the eighteenth-century inhabitants of Havana knew that an error might have been made, and they welcomed the relics with all due pomp and reverence. On 15 January 1796 the *San Lorenzo* sailed into the harbour with its precious cargo, and four days later three boats were rowed abreast, slowly and with muffled oars, to the shore. The central one bore a coffin swathed in black velvet, decorated with golden embroidery, tassels and fringes and guarded by sailors in deep mourning.

This coffin was carried solemnly to the Plaza de Armas and laid on a carved and gilded ebony throne, placed in turn on a vast bier, also covered in black velvet and lit by forty-two candles. The coffin was reverently opened. Inside it lay the small lead casket, gilded and fastened with an iron lock. The lid was lifted in the sight of the governor general, but it was disappointedly related that all that remained of the 'incomparable Almirante Cristóbal Colón'[9] was a pathetic little pile of dust and a piece of bone.

The casket was replaced, and the nobles, soldiers, priests and people of Havana processed to the cathedral, while salutes were fired from the fortresses and bells rang from the Castillo de la Real Fuerza and all the churches. Each of the noblemen took it in turn to savour the honour of holding one of the golden tassels on the bier for a few moments as the procession moved slowly along. Finally it arrived at the cathedral, the interior of which was entirely draped in mourning, with black banners hanging on its columns. After a ceremonial mass had been said in a blaze of candlelight, the casket was placed in a niche in the wall. This was sealed with a marble slab, on which was inscribed:

> O remains and image of the great Columbus!
> For a thousand ages stay preserved in this urn
> In remembrance of our nation.[10]

The garden in the patio of the
Seminario de San Carlos y San Ambrosio.

6

HAVANA BESIEGED AND CAPTURED

'This great Island is easie to be conquer'd … they much dread an old Prophecy amongst them, viz. that within a short time the English will as freely walk the streets of Havana, as the Spaniards now do.'

Major Smith, Governor of the Island of Providence[1]

EARLY IN MAY 1762 MARTIN de Arana set out on one of the secret trips that he often made between Cuba and Jamaica. Although no Cuban was supposed to trade with any country but Spain, many people bent the law to swell their personal coffers, and Don Martín was no exception. Clothing was his line, and each illicit run to Jamaica made him a tidy profit, well worth the risk of being caught.

When he arrived in Kingston he knew immediately that something odd was going on; the town was in an abnormal state of noise and bustle. Carts laden with boxes and bundles were being driven to the harbour. The streets were full of sailors. Vessels jostled against the wharves, where gangs of sweating slaves were stacking ominous quantities of military equipment and ammunition. De Arana went to see some Jewish merchants with whom he had dealt in the past to find out what was afoot. They confirmed his worst fears. The ships that were being so hurriedly prepared and provisioned were soon to sail under Sir James Douglas to rendezvous with an even greater force. The British were preparing to attack Havana.

The Jews told de Arana that a total ban had been put on civilian travel, both out of Kingston and the island, but even under a dual risk – first of being caught breaking the ban and second of exposing his own activities to the Spanish authorities – de Arana decided that it was his duty

The Castillo del los Tres Santos
Reyes Magos del Morro
from the Battery of the Twelve Apostles.

to return to Havana to warn its citizens of the impending assault. Cautious enquiries elicited the information that a small vessel was shortly to leave from a creek along the coast on an illegal trading run. After making a detailed report of everything that he had seen and heard and hiding the paper in his shirt, de Arana went to see the captain and talked his way on board the boat.

They sailed northwest towards the Yucatán Straits. De Arana was put ashore at Cabo Corrientes, the second most westerly point of the island of Cuba. He knew that he was still faced with a lengthy journey which he had no hope of making on foot if he was to arrive in time to avert disaster. There was not a soul to be seen, and all he had brought for sustenance was a loaf of bread and a pot of honey. However, rather than hang about wringing his hands, he set off into the surrounding woods, shouting as he went to attract someone's attention.

The area was almost deserted, but eventually he was found, thirsty and hoarse, by a Negro pig-farmer. When he heard de Arana's story the man instantly agreed to help him. The smuggler and his rescuer had to make another long, hot walk in quite the wrong direction as the nearest farm was on the other side of a wide bay at Cabo San Antonio. An agonizing delay ensued while delicate negotiations were undertaken with the owner of a horse, who was most reluctant to part with it. Eventually de Arana was able to set off on a long, difficult ride through the swamps and mountains to Havana.

After many days he arrived in the city. He made straight for the Castillo de la Real Fuerza, the residence of the governor, Don Juan de Prado Malleza y Portocarrero de Luna. He slid off his horse and stumbled over the drawbridge. Covered with sweat and dust, and almost fainting with hunger and exhaustion, he gasped out to the guards that he had news of the first importance to convey to the governor. To his despair, they flatly refused to admit him. When de Arana began to shout at them the governor's secretary, José García Gayó, came out of his office to discover the cause of the disturbance. Almost incoherent with relief, de Arana poured out his tale, but the secretary merely gave him a long stare through narrowed eyes, and asked him whether he could possibly be expected to believe the cock-and-bull story of a smuggler who was clearly trying to divert the governor's attention away from his own crimes. Better in a cell, the secretary thought, and he told the guards to arrest de Arana.

This exchange had been overheard by Don Martín de Ulloa, the military secretary. De Ulloa suspected that there might be something in the story. He took de Arana to his own house, gave him something to drink, and asked him to repeat all the details. Considerably alarmed, de Ulloa went back to the Fuerza, walked straight into the governor's room and told him what de Arana had said. Juan de Prado was a field-marshal, but his reactions to this and to future warnings of the British approach were unsoldierly. He refused even to hear Martín de Ulloa out. De Ulloa went home frustrated and tried in vain to console his distraught guest.

A couple of weeks later the governor and his officials were uncomfortably sweltering through a mass celebrating the festival of the Holy Trinity when a messenger came into the church. The news was that a great crowd of sails had been seen off the coast. Juan de Prado was not concerned. There was no cause for alarm, it was just a passing convoy. The governor went to see for himself and considered his opinion confirmed. When he saw Martín de Arana talking to de Ulloa and some colleagues, he asked: 'What is it, Señor de Arana?' 'What else can it be, Sir,' de Arana replied, 'but that which I faced so many hardships to report to you fifteen days ago, as a dutiful vassal of the king and a good Spaniard.'[2]

No sooner had the governor returned to his rooms in the Castillo de la Real Fuerza than the news was brought to him that soldiers were embarking from the 'friendly convoy' for the shore, beginning what for Juan de Prado was to be the most catastrophic event of his career.

In 1752 a new British governor, Charles Knowles, had been appointed to the island of Jamaica. A few years afterwards the Cuban governor extended an official invitation to him to pay a visit to Havana. The offer was accepted with pleasure, and the guest spent much of his stay carefully memorizing the details of Havana's defences. Later he wrote down all his observations in a report which he sent to London.

Knowles's sharp eyes were soon to stand his government in good stead. Five years after the beginning of the Seven Years' War, pressure from the French, combined with anti-British sentiment exacerbated by British maritime aggression in the New World, caused Carlos III to sign a pact with France against England. On 4 January 1762 George III declared war on Spain. The plan for an attack on Havana, previously drawn up by the Duke of Cumberland, using information from Knowles's report, was presented to the government. The plan was approved, and preparations were swiftly put in hand. The expedition would afford an opportunity to seize one of Spain's most important possessions and disrupt her activities in the Caribbean. It was also likely to be highly lucrative.

George Keppel, third Earl
of Albemarle.

Major-General the Hon.
William Keppel.

106

Rear-Admiral the Hon.
Augustus Keppel.

There were various frustrating delays before departure, not the least of which was the discovery that much of the bedding intended for the expedition was either rotten or had been eaten by rats. The vessels finally sailed from Spithead on 6 March. The command of the fleet was given to Sir George Pocock, who had enjoyed a distinguished career since joining the navy at the age of twelve. George Keppel, third Earl of Albemarle, was given the command of the troops, less on his merits than because he was a favourite of the Duke of Cumberland under whom he had served. Albemarle was not popular. James Wolfe sneeringly branded him 'one of those showy men who are seen in palaces … [who] never desires to see his regiment.'[3] His appointment was seen as controversial, especially as his brothers Augustus and William Keppel were also given positions of command on the expedition. Like his brother, William had served on Cumberland's staff, and he was sent to Havana as a major-general. In their portraits both he and Albemarle look plump and prosperous in their glamorous uniforms, but Augustus looks stern, beetle-browed and craggy. He was well fitted by his naval experience for his appointment as Pocock's commodore.

Governor Juan de Prado's lack of concern at the approach of the fleet was symptomatic of the fact that the citizens of Havana had, since the construction of the forts, been resting on their laurels. Havana was reputed to be well-defended. The castles of the Morro, Fuerza and Punta looked impressive, but in the summer of 1762 the city was inadequately prepared for anything as ambitious and well-organized as the British plan of attack. There was an acute shortage of weapons and ammunition. The summer months usually saw an acceleration of disease, and by the time the British approached the city its garrison had been severely reduced by an epidemic of yellow fever.

The most dangerous deficiency in Havana's defences was the absence of any fortification on the Cabaña. It was obvious to many people that this long ridge, which overlooks not only the harbour and the city but also the Castillo del Morro, was a strategic site of tremendous value. During the construction of the Morro the engineer, Giovanni Baptista Antonelli, had climbed up the Cabaña. When he saw the view from the top he exclaimed that whoever controlled the hill would control Havana. King Carlos had repeatedly asked Juan de Prado to do something about fortifying it, but, true to form, the governor had hardly lifted a finger.

Soon after mass was over in Havana on 6 June, de Prado suffered a rude awakening. Even he could no longer deny that the approaching vessels were carrying far too many soldiers to be a 'friendly convoy'. The British force consisted of over 11,000 troops and several hundred Negro slaves.

The fleet commanded by Sir George Pocock during the siege consisted of ten ships of between seventy and ninety guns each: *Cambridge, Centaur, Culloden, Dragon, Dublin, Marlborough, Namur, Temeraire, Temple* and *Valiant*; twelve ships of between sixty and seventy guns each: *Alcide, Belleisle, Defiance, Devonshire, Edgar, Hampton Court, Intrepid, Nottingham, Orford, Pembroke, Ripon* and *Stirling Castle*; four ships of fifty guns each; *Centurion, Deptford, Hampshire* and *Sutherland*; three frigates of around forty guns each: *Dover, Enterprize* and *Penzance*; seven frigates of between twenty-eight and thirty-two guns each: *Alarm, Boreas, Cerberus, Echo, Lizard, Richmond* and *Trent*; five frigates of around twenty guns each: *Fowey, Glasgow, Mercury, Port Mahon* and *Rose*; nine smaller vessels of between fourteen and sixteen guns each: *Barbadoes, Bonetta, Cygnet, Ferret, Lurcher, Merlin, Porcupine, Port Royal* and *Viper*; three bomb ketches of eight guns each: *Basilisk, Grenado* and *Thunder*, and many store, hospital, transport and supply vessels.

Everyone in Havana could see what was in the offing, and de Prado was forced to admit his mistake. That evening he called a council of war to decide what was to be done to prevent the Key to the New World falling into enemy hands. The garrison was put on the alert; every fit man in Havana was summoned to fight; 9,000 sailors from the visiting ships were detailed to the defence; the patchy armaments were supplemented with pikes and machetes; and the governor pressed the city's slaves into service, holding out the possibility of liberty as an incentive.

The British drew closer. They knew that their numbers far outweighed those of Havana's garrison, having obtained information from the crews of some Spanish vessels that they had successfully attacked *en route*. One ship had evaded their grasp. Had she put back to Havana fast enough, the city might have been given time to become better prepared, if, that is, her news could have made any impression on Governor de Prado's bovine serenity.

Pocock had taken great care to surprise the Habaneros. After collecting troops in Martinique he chose to sail to the city through the treacherous waters of the Bahama Channel northeast of Cuba rather than be seen approaching along the easier western route. It was remarkable that the fleet reached Havana at all, given the uselessness of the pilots who had been sent from New Providence in the Bahamas. One of them, James Kimblin, 'tho old and dim-sighted' was 'still reputed with the help of his glass to be well qualified for that service, and has voluntarily offered himself'.[4] The poor old pilot, obviously longing for a bit of glory, was among those sent home late in June by the admiral. They were accompanied by a letter in which Pocock remarked tartly that 'out of the ten men sent with Captain Holmes under the denomination of pilots, very few were in any measure capable of conducting ships through the Old Straits of Bahama, neither did they pretend to be qualified for pilots.'[5] To get his larger vessels through the channel, Pocock had to have soundings taken and fires lit on the numerous cays (reefs) with which it is littered.

The British arrived off Cojímar, to the east of Havana. Augustus Keppel gathered his crew together and, waving his hat in a fever of excitement, shouted: 'Courage, my lads! The day is ours. The Admiral has given us leave to take yonder town, with all the treasure in it… We shall all be as rich as Jews. The place is paved with gold.'[6] The men responded with three wild cheers.

The following day, 7 June, landings began before dawn east of the Morro near the River Cojímar, covered by the *Dragon, Temeraire, Valiant, Pembroke, Ripon, Dover, Richmond, Trent, Mercury, Bonetta, Grenado, Thunder* and *Basilisk*. Under the command of Augustus Keppel, 3,963 troops embarked in flat-bottomed boats at six o'clock under strict instructions 'not to make the least noise by huzzaing'.[7] The first wave landed at half past ten. The little stone fort at Cojímar, after being 'very well cannonaded'[8] by the *Dragon, Bonetta* and *Mercury*, was abandoned by the peasants and Negroes defending it. A party of British troops seized the fort and crossed the River Cojímar.

The soldiers spent the night on a little sandy beach nearby. It had been a trying day of wild gales, lightning and thunderclaps. By evening the rain was crashing down in torrents. The troops did not sleep well, Commodore Keppel had a splitting headache, and everybody must have thought longingly of their cosy British beds.

On 8 June the troops marched south of the bay to the village of Guanabacoa. They encountered little resistance from its inhabitants, although later the harassment of the British by one of the local officials, José Antonio Gómez de Bullones, caused a certain amount of inconvenience. Pepe Antonio, as he was affectionately known, was soon designated one of the heroes of the event. His machete is still lovingly preserved in the Museum of Guanabacoa, despite the fact that the British took the village in time for lunch.

HORENDOY TERRIBLE COMBATE QVE TVBO LA NACION BRITANICA EN EL CASTILLO DEL MORRO, DEL QVE
ERA COMANDANTE Dⁿ LVIS VIZENTE DE VELASCO CAPITAN DE NAVIO DELA REAL ARMADA DE S.M.C.

PLANO. DEL PVERTOLCIVDAD DELA HAVANA SITIADO Pᴿ LAS ARMAS DE S.M.B. EL DIA 7 DE JVNIO DE 1762 SIENDO SV GOBERNⁿADOR
EL MARISC. DE CAMPO Dⁿ JVAN DE PRADO I COMANDⁿ DELA ESQVADRA EL GEFE Dⁿ GUTIEREZ DE EVIA Y Qⁿ MANDAVA LA ESQVADRA INGLESA EL ALMIRAL JORGE POCOK

A Spanish depiction of 'Havana besieged by the forces of His Britannic Majesty'.

A plate from the *London Magazine*, 1762.

110

Within Havana's walls there was terrible panic. An order was given that all the women and children should leave the city. This produced a headlong rush through the gates that caused the roads to become jammed, adding to the general terror and confusion. The council desperately tried to devise a plan to defend Havana against the onslaught that now appeared inevitable. The Castillo del Morro lacked a commander, so the job was given to the captain of the *Reina*, one of the ships then at anchor in the port. The choice of Don Luís Vicente de Velasco Isla was one of the few sensible decisions made by the Spanish throughout the whole campaign. He was placed, with his second-in-command, the Marqués Vicente de González, at the head of 350 soldiers, 50 sailors and 300 slaves. He resolved to defend the Morro faithfully, if necessary with his dying breath. The courage and ability with which Luís de Velasco was to fulfil his intention was not matched by the actions of his fellow-defenders. Following a decision by the council, three ships, *Neptuno, Asia* and *Europa*, were sunk in the harbour mouth. The object was to keep the British out, but the Spanish had, in their ill-considered haste, trapped their own warships in the port.

The harbour mouth, showing the masts
of the wrecked Spanish ships.

On the night of 8 June the British began to reconnoitre the foot of the Cabaña. The Spanish soldiers stationed there could hear but not see them, and they took to firing wildly in all directions. The crews of the Spanish men-of-war in the harbour assumed that the shots were an enemy attack. They turned their guns on the hill and began to fire at their colleagues, a display of ineptitude that continued until one o'clock in the morning. The troops on the Cabaña then surpassed themselves by abandoning their posts, pausing only to throw their precious guns into the harbour.

On the evening of 9 June a deserter walked into the British camp. He told the British that the people of Havana were tired and frightened to death. The commanders' ears pricked up when he added that the fleet from Veracruz, carrying 14 million pesos, was due to arrive any day. When evening fell on 10 June, Admiral Pocock commanded a bombardment of the fort of Santa Dorotea de Luna de la Chorrera to the west of Havana, the woods along the adjoining coastline and the northern part of the city. At dawn, boatloads of marines made for the shore as though a major landing was soon to take place. Don Luís de Aguiar, the commander of the Chorrera, had been unable to continue its defence under the hail of British bombardment. When a few of the marines landed at noon, they were able to occupy the fort without delay.

As the cannonballs rained down on them the Habaneros must have felt that all hell was breaking loose, and this was precisely what the enemy commanders intended. The attack on the Chorrera and bombardment of the city were only overtures intended to distract Spanish attention from the main performance planned for that night: the capture of the Cabaña. Possession of the hill was now vital. 'There is no other ground from where the place can be attacked with like advantage,' Admiral Knowles had written, 'and, in marching up to it, I don't apprehend the troops can be annoyed from the Morro.'[9]

By about half past two on the afternoon of 11 June this vital strategic prize, upon which the Spanish had only just thought to place a few cannon, had been taken with very little more bother than the forts at Cojímar and the Chorrera. During the attack it began to pour with rain. Pocock thought that 'the shower must be in the faces of the enemy and that would be of favour to our troops,'[10] but the British did not need the help of the elements. The Spanish simply ran away as they approached. That night the British took soundings along the north face of the Morro. They found that the water there was quite deep enough for large ships to

The British had no prior intelligence of the great depth of the Morro's dry moat.

sail in and bombard it. However, it was so dark that even when Captain John Barker of the *Culloden* sneaked in 'so nigh that I heard the sentinels speak',[11] he could not estimate the height of the walls.

So far, the British plan was running smoothly. The Habaneros had been placed in an almost impossible predicament. The enemy had established themselves to the east, south and west, and the Spanish ships hemmed inside the harbour could make no move against the enemy's dominant position along the northern coast. Furthermore, the loss of the Cabaña meant that the citizens of Havana were at the potential mercy of the British guns. They did not know which way to turn.

Luís de Velasco, the commander of the Morro, kept his head. The British had begun to construct batteries on the Cabaña, and de Velasco directed steady fire at them, which was backed up by the ships in the harbour. The weather was becoming hotter. The British troops struggled under the broiling sun to drag heavy cannon up the beach and along rough roads to the Cabaña. They also had to transport soil to build the batteries, as the rock on top of the

A fanciful French depiction of
the attack on Havana.

hill was almost bare. Any men who strayed away from the main working parties were seized by 'the enemy's wild horsemen'[12] who killed them and left British bodies 'mangled to pieces'[13] for their comrades to find. Heat, thirst and fatigue began to take their toll.

Meanwhile, de Velasco took care to keep his men's spirits up. He encouraged them when they felt their cause was lost and set up a rota in which every man was replaced by reserves from the city every few days, in order that the Morro's defenders would not become tired and lose their edge. De Velasco knew that if he were able to prolong the situation long enough either hardship, disease or the start of the hurricane season would put the British at a crucial disadvantage. The British knew it too. Despite de Velasco's efforts, however, the batteries were progressing, and when on 29 June the Spanish attempted a pre-dawn raid on the Cabaña hundreds of them were killed, wounded and taken prisoner. The total of British killed or wounded was ten.

The only circumstance to mar the enemy's pleasure at the fiasco was the absence of the treasure-laden fleet from Veracruz. Keppel and Pocock decided that Juan de Prado must somehow have alerted its commanders, although Commodore Augustus Keppel remarked that 'Spanish sloth and stupidity is so unaccountable that I begin to think nothing impossible that relates to their actions'.[14]

By 1 July everything had been made ready, and the British were poised to attack the Morro. Albemarle's men bombarded it from the landward side with over forty cannon and mortars, while the *Cambridge, Marlborough* and *Dragon* under Captain Augustus Hervey fired on its northern face. For some time thick clouds of smoke obscured the view from the ships, but as it slowly drifted away it became obvious that the height of the Morro's walls had been underestimated. The British fire was striking too low to achieve any real damage. Shots from the Morro, on the other hand, had destroyed the ships' masts, sails and rigging. Five hours later, after Captain Goostrey of the *Cambridge* and many of his crew had been killed, the ships were recalled.

The British situation began to look gloomy. No matter how much damage their batteries did to the Morro, de Velasco always managed to repair the holes in the walls with wood and to keep up a brisk return of fire. British stocks of ammunition were running low, and on 2 July Pocock wrote to Albemarle: 'I am apt to think El Morro will not be given up until Don Velasco cannot maintain it a moment longer than his force will admit.'[15]

The British situation became progressively worse. Food supplies were running out and there was a desperate need for water. Disease began to run riot among the troops, and every day saw rising numbers of deaths from yellow fever, dysentery and thirst. Some 8,000 of the men were sick, but proper care was almost impossible, and medical supplies were rapidly diminishing. Many of the sufferers were simply rotting alive, and quantities of corpses floated in the sea. James Miller, a soldier who served in the campaign, later related that: 'The fatigues on shore were excessive, the bad water brought on disorders, which were mortal, you would see the men's tongues, hanging out parched like a mad dog's.'[16] The commanders were also suffering from illness and anxiety. Augustus Keppel thought that his brother Albemarle would 'fatigue himself into a sickness'.[17] Clearly something had to be done, or the climate would defeat the British before they could beat the Spaniards.

Inside the Morro, Luís de Velasco and his comparatively tiny force of men were undergoing even greater hardships. Many of them had been killed or wounded during the bombardment from land and sea. The survivors, despite the arrival of reinforcements from the city, were exhausted. The fort had been severely damaged, and half its watchtower had been shot away. De Velasco had had to return briefly to the city to rest and receive treatment for a shoulder wound. The British commanders had conceived a tremendous respect for his tenacity, in the face of which the only option left to them was to blast their way into the fort. They set about mining its walls on 17 July. 'El Morro,' Albemarle had declared, 'we must and will have'.[18]

By 29 July, in spite of Spanish attempts to hinder the process, the mines were set in place. Albemarle sent de Velasco a long letter, begging him to give up his determination to meet a hero's death. Although the Morro's commander remained fixed in his resolve, he responded graciously:

The treaty of capitulation that Your Excellency has invited me to draw up, with the advantages that this honour bestows upon me, is one of the estimable characteristics that Your Excellency displays to your possible prisoners, a sign of your great gallantry.... I do not aspire to immortalize my name, I only wish to pour out my last breath in the defence of my monarch, and the motivation for my actions is in no small part dictated by the honour due to my nation and by love of my homeland.... I only know of one reason for which I must thank my lucky star: the high honour in which I may be held in being remembered as being one of your devoted servants.[19]

The following afternoon, Albemarle ordered the mines to be sprung. The ear-splitting blast seemed to the Habaneros to shake the entire city. It tore an enormous hole in the walls, through which an avalanche of masonry, cannon and men's bodies cascaded over the rocks. The British burst through the breach into the fort. An hour of the most bloodthirsty hand-to-hand fighting took place. Musket shots rang round the walls, and the air was full of smoke and the agonized cries of the wounded and dying. The ground ran with gore. Through the scene of flying blades and struggling bodies the Marqués de González could be glimpsed, standing with his back to the flag, furiously slashing at his attackers. But at the next moment he fell dead at the foot of the flagpole, his body hacked and bleeding. De Velasco was shot in the chest and received a horrible sword-cut, but continued to fight until his strength was sapped and he sank fainting to the ground, his elegant uniform sodden with blood.

The Castillo del Morro had fallen. About 400 of its defenders had been slain, 400 more

'The Breach of the Morro Castle by Storm – 30 July 1762'.

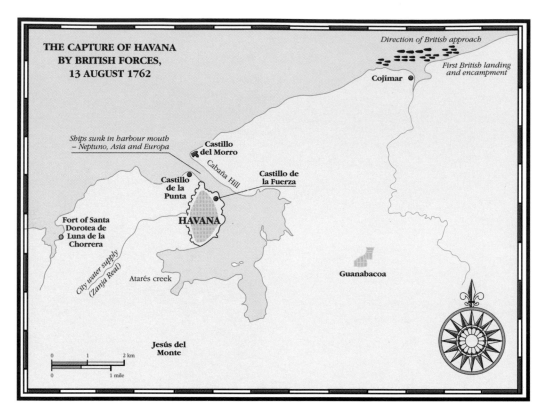

THE CAPTURE OF HAVANA
BY BRITISH FORCES,
13 AUGUST 1762

Direction of British approach

*First British landing
and encampment*

Cojímar

*Ships sunk in harbour mouth
– Neptuno, Asia and Europa*

Castillo
del Morro

Cabaña Hill

Castillo de
la Fuerza

Castillo
de la
Punta

Fort of Santa
Dorotea de
Luna de la
Chorrera

HAVANA

*City water supply
(Zanja Real)*

Atarés creek

Guanabacoa

Jesús del
Monte

0   1   2 km

0   1 mile

The Spanish flag taken from
the Morro, 30 July 1762.

118

were taken prisoner, and many men were drowned trying to get across the bay to safety. 'The city was inexpressibly grieved at the loss of the Morro,' wrote a Jesuit priest who lived in Havana at the time. 'It was at four o'clock in the afternoon, and those who saw the flag of St George fluttering from the fort were unable to believe it.'[20] Luís de Velasco asked to be taken to Havana to be treated by a Spanish doctor. Albemarle readily granted his request and sent an officer with him, with instructions that if for any reason this was not possible he should be brought back to the British side, in order that he might be given 'all the care and homage that was due to an officer who, with so much glory, had known how to uphold his trust and the honour of his Prince's arms'.[21]

De Velasco's lung had not been damaged by the shot, but when they observed his increasing fever and delirium the doctors set to with a will to dig the ball out from his chest. The infection that resulted from this operation delivered the final blow; on 31 July Don Luís de Velasco was given the last rites and died in the arms of his young nephew, the ensign Don Santiago Muñoz de Velasco. A cease-fire was ordered by both sides for Velasco's burial, and when the British heard the crack of a salute being fired during the funeral procession they echoed it with a tribute from their own guns across the bay.

A few days earlier, long-awaited reinforcements to the British side had begun to arrive from North America, and fresh supplies were sent from Jamaica. The enemy's morale lifted. By 1 August a hill at Jesús del Monte directly south of the city had been taken. The waters of the Zanja Real had been diverted away from the city, and now flowed uselessly into the Atarés creek, one of the branches of the harbour.

Havana was surrounded, without food or water. Even if the number of volleys fired were strictly controlled, there was enough ammunition to last for only a few days. A last ditch attempt was made to fire at the cistern of the Morro, in order to deprive the enemy of water, but it failed. Nobody had much faith in the city walls' ability to withstand further assault. The governor recorded that they were not high or thick enough, they were too narrow to take sufficient troops to repel a ladder attack, and they were too weak to stand up to heavy bombardment. Havana's much-vaunted fortifications were proving unequal to their defensive task. On 2 August more North American troops joined the enemy forces. By the 10th over double the original number of British guns were trained on the city. Albemarle wrote to the governor:

Sir, My dispositions for the reduction of the Havana are made. Motives of humanity induce me to acquaint Your Excellency therewith, that you may have an opportunity of making your proposals to surrender the Havana to His Britannic Majesty, and thereby prevent the fatal calamities which always attend the storming of a town. No one can be more averse to the shedding of blood than I am; to prevent it as much as in my power, I desire Your Excellency to consider that however my disposition may incline to humanity, it may not be possible to extend its influence to the preservation of your troops in a manner they so recently experienced at the reduction of El Morro. I am master of La Cabaña and El Morro, which Your Excellency, in a letter to Don Luis de Velasco, acknowledges to be the key to the Havana. … Should Your Excellency want passports or escorts for ladies who are at present in the town, I shall most readily send them to you.[22]

However, Juan de Prado, with Velasco's example before him and the citizens staunchly urging further resistance, replied:

Most Excellent Sir: The natural and sworn obligations which oblige me to defend this place (with which the King, my master, has had the goodness to trust me) with all the efforts which are regular and common on such an occasion for officers of honour who would execute their duty faithfully … does not permit me to condescend to the proposal Your Excellency makes me in this day's letter concerning the giving up of this place … I find myself well assured of carrying on the defence, with strong hopes of a happy exit, and capable of preserving it under the dominion of His Most Catholic Majesty, to whom it belongs, which is my constant care. … In regard to passports Your Excellency offers to the ladies, I acknowledge your polite attention.[23]

On the following morning every British gun began to thunder on Havana. By midday the defenders of the city had only a few hours' ammunition left. At two o'clock white flags were hung out from the Punta and along the walls, and the governor sent a second letter to Albemarle:

Dear Sir: The considerations of humanity which Your Excellency did me the honour of setting before me in your letter of yesterday's date, reinforced by the appeals and representations made to me on behalf of the public of this city which for so long has undergone the evil consequences resulting from operations of war, have induced me to modify the intention I had formed of continuing the defence of the city to the last extremity, as I explained to Your Excellency in my reply to Your Excellency's afore-mentioned letter. They provide reasons for me now to entreat you to direct that these operations of war be suspended for twenty-four hours, so that I may issue directions concerning them, and prepare, for transmission to Your Excellency, the Articles of Capitulation that will permit the city to be surrendered.[24]

The British agreed to the cease-fire. However, when the commanders read the governor's proposed articles of capitulation, which suggested that the ships in the harbour should remain in Spanish possession, they were furious. On 12 August a threatening message was returned:

> Most Excellent Sir: We have had translated and perused a few of the Articles of Capitulation Your Excellency sent us and find them so repugnant to the customs of war and your present situation that we are under a necessity of returning them, and desire if it is your real intention to capitulate that you will please to send an officer fully empowered to treat of the surrender upon such terms as shall appear to us reasonable to grant. We desire this officer may be here by six o'clock this evening, otherwise at that time the suspension of arms will cease.[25]

The people were unable to bear the prospect of further loss of life and damage to the city. On 13 August Havana was surrendered to the enemy commanders. They were delighted to find the warehouses crammed with valuable goods, including 5,842 chests of sugar, 4,876 bales of snuff, 3,384 bales of cocoa, 123 bales of quinine, 8,000 uncured hides, 4,000 tanned hides and 500 bales of tobacco. All of this, together with one fifth of the Spanish fleet which was lying at anchor in the harbour, passed into their possession. The combined value of the spoils amounted to £3 million.

The conquerors of the city graciously permitted the Spanish troops to leave Havana with the honours of war. However, when the ex-governor, Juan de Prado, reached Spain he was sentenced to life imprisonment for the dishonourable and bungling behaviour that had hastened the loss of Havana. The memory of Luís Vicente de Velasco was honoured by the bestowal of the title of Marqueses del Morro on the future heads of his family, and the vow, which has never been broken, that from thenceforth there would always be a vessel in the Spanish navy called *Velasco.*

When the news of Havana's downfall reached England and her colonies there were great demonstrations of delight. The victory was trumpeted in the newspapers. Lord Albemarle, Admiral Pocock and Commodore Keppel became instant celebrities. Bonfires were lit and parties were given. Popular ballads were penned in honour of the triumph.

THE HAVANNAH'S GARLAND

A new Song on the taking of Havannah, to the tune of Boyn-water

1

GIVE Ear, true Britons to my Song,
And joyful Acclamations:
'Tis the noble Deeds now done,
By our own Relations.
While Albemarle did command
Pocock and General Keppel:
Let Moro Fort, and Spaniards vaunt,
If Britons be unable.

2

Against Havannah we set sail,
With a fleet of Combination,
Land troops we likewise had on Board,
To pay of Spain's Aggression.
We moor'd our ships, and landed our Troops,
The Spaniards came down raging;
But they found we were true British Boys,
As we their Fury were swaging.

3

We chac'd the Spaniards thro' the Woods,
And hunted them like Mawkin,
And turn'd up Hundreds in their Suds,
The rest ran Homeward quaking.
For though they came in thousands on,
Our Fire would make them scatter;
But we true Britons kept our Ground,
While blood did run like Water.

4

The Spaniards judg'd the Moro's Fort,
The Britains' Strength would banter;
But when we blew it up i' the Air,
They turn'd another Chanter.
Bold Harvey with three noble Ships,
Their Walls by Sea did batter,
While we bombarded it by Land,
And did their Out-works chatter.

5

But never was heard such woful Thuds,
As the Cambridge and Malborough:
The Dragon fired as brisk as they,
But for Smoak none could perceive them.
The Cambridge got her Captain shot,
And a hundred more beside him:
Brave Harvey then his Station quit,
For long five hours he try'd them.

6

But finding it Bomb and Cannon-proof,
We then did give it over,
And sprung a Mine below their Walls,
Which split the Rocks in Shivers.
Some Spaniards went up wi' the Blast,
Which made their Fellows wonder:
Such a hideous Roar ne'er heard before,
It far exceeded Thunder.

7

Then we approached upon a Breach,
Our Firelocks cock'd and ready:
Where the Spaniards met us for a brush,
Imploring on their Lady.
To aid Valasco a Spaniard bold,
A valiant Sea commander,
Who vow'd for to defend that Fort,
While Marza kept up his Standard.

8

O then began the bloody Fray,
With Bayonets and broad Swords champing:
Thro' Bones and Bellies we made our way,
And dying Men under us trampling,
Of seven hundred Spaniards here,
Scarce left alive was eighty:
Valasco by his Standard fell,
Whose Deeds were counted mighty.

9

Then to Havannah we did march,
And trenches rais'd like Mountains;
Then cut away their Water Pipes,
Which supply'd them with fresh Fountains
Our Batteries then began to play,
With Roars aloud like Thunder,
Which dash'd their Walls and Chimnies down,
Yet loath for to knock under.

10

O then with Bombs and fiery Balls
Threaten'd their utter Ruin
Which rais'd such Cries, as pierced the Skies,
For Mercy they were suing;
Jurro de Prado to British Terms
Was loath to be subjected,
But brave Albemarle told him his Fate,
Was then to be ransacked.

11

Or buried in the City's Ruin,
Him and his whole Fraternity;
This made him to Subjection yield,
And so they were disarmed;
All stores and treasures of the place
Are bought by Briton's Glory,
Seven Ships, their Arms, and every Thing,
And that is a noble story.

12

O then with Honour we lin'd their Gates,
And bravery to our wishing,
And turn'd Don Spaniards from their posts,
Which they held by Commission:
May our noble King prosper long,
And all his brave Commanders,
Who bravely led on Britain's Sons
To knock down Popish Standards.

Delight in England contrasted sharply with Spanish anxiety, and the poor pawns in Havana were distraught. The Marquesa de Jústiz de Santa Ana, in a poetic version of a long protest that the women of the city sent to Carlos III, wrote:

Thou, Havana, capitulated?	How many can show the signs,
Thou in tears? Thou exterminated?	The scars and wounds,
Thou now under foreign domination?	Received for thee, Havana?
O Sorrow, adored homeland!	Only the hospitals can tell
How many sacrificed themselves	If all the evils of active engagement
To prevent thy alienation?	Were the objects of our desire,
And how many more envied	But subjected as we were to bombardment
The happy and honourable fortune	Our action was but passive
Of marking thy passing	And without sufficient arms
With a bloody death?	We became a trophy of our enemies.[26]

In twentieth-century Havana, indirect reference is still made to the British presence in the city. If an Habanero knows that something dire is about to happen – perhaps he has received an ominously worded summons to see his boss, or his wife's best friend has seen him with his mistress – he will remark in doom-laden tones that 'now is the hour of the mameyes'. Mameyes are tropical fruit with vermilion flesh and shiny black seeds, the same colours as the uniforms of the invaders in 1762. The saying *Ha llegado la hora de los mameyes* relates directly to the occupation of Havana by the British, whose commanders did extremely well out of the expedition. Pocock and Albemarle each received shares of £122,697, while the latter's private soldiers got £4. Once established in Havana, however, Albemarle became greedy. Many law suits were brought against him by merchants on whom he attempted to levy illegal taxes.

In the long term, the economic aspect of the British occupation proved beneficial to Havana. The tight trade restrictions that the Spanish had imposed were lifted, and the harbour soon became crowded with merchant ships of many nationalities. But in the short term the British appeared to be bent on milking the sad city dry. Some of Havana's inhabitants, such as Don Sebastián Peñalver de Angulo who lived in the Palacio de los Marqueses de Aguas Claras in the Plaza de la Catedral, found it expedient to collaborate with their new

124

Ha llegado la hora de los mameyes:
William Keppel at the Morro
by Sir Joshua Reynolds.

masters, but this behaviour was anathema to those in whom loyalty, devout Catholicism and wounded pride combined into a bitter loathing of the British.

The Bishop of Cuba, Don Pedro Agustín Morell de Santa Cruz de Lora, was one Habanero who steadfastly refused to acknowledge the conquerors' superiority. After the occupation of the city one of the first actions of Lieutenant-Colonel Samuel Cleaveland, the commander of the artillery, was to demand a list of all the bells in the churches, monasteries, convents and sugar plantations. He further required the specifications of the metals from which they were cast so that he could assess the amount of the cash payment, equivalent to their value, that he expected to be given. The bishop, who would have done anything rather than cooperate with the invaders, made Cleaveland a grudging offer of 1,000 pesos. The Colonel, knowing well that this was a ridiculous estimate, swiftly returned a demand for 30,000 pesos. Don Pedro, becoming more obstinate by the minute, refused to contemplate the idea of such a sum. Albemarle was forced to intervene. He wrote in rather shaky Castilian to the bishop on 27 August: 'Illustrious Sir, the payment offered to the officer in command of H.M. Artillery ... is so negligible that I am obliged to demonstrate my disgust.'[27] He recommended that Cleaveland be paid 10,000 pesos.

Don Pedro then tried a different tack. He pleaded poverty, telling the irritated officers that he would have to take up a collection. One can imagine the delight with which the people would have contributed to this cause – the amount raised was a laughable 103 pesos. Finally Cleaveland lost his temper and set an early deadline, leaving Don Pedro with no alternative but to pay.

Meanwhile, another row was brewing between the Commander and the bishop. On 30 August Albemarle sent Don Pedro a letter asking that one of the city's churches be set aside for British worship. The bishop sent a long, procrastinatory reply. Albemarle, becoming seriously annoyed, wrote again on 4 September telling Don Pedro that it would be better for him if he did as he was asked, instead of exhausting himself in writing such lengthy screeds. Ultimately Albemarle decided to choose a church himself. The bishop replied in an aggrieved tone that since the noble earl had come to that conclusion, he might as well take whichever one he pleased. This proved to be that of San Francisco de Asís in the Plaza de San Francisco. After being commandeered by the British, it was never again used for worship by the citizens of Havana.

H A V A N A – *Portrait of a City*

Albemarle's chosen church:
the Iglesia de San Francisco de Asís.

Albemarle's chosen church: the Iglesia de San Francisco de Asís.

Albemarle then plunged into a concerted campaign of bishop-baiting.

Most Illustrious Sir: I am sorry to be under the necessity of writing to your Lordship what ought to have been thought of some days ago, viz., a donation from the church to the Commander-in-Chief of the victorious army. The least that your Lordship can offer will be 100,000 pesos. I wish to live in peace with your Lordship and the church, as I have shown in all that has hitherto occurred, and I hope that your Lordship will not give me reason to alter my intention. I kiss your Lordship's hands.

Your humble servant

ALBEMARLE.

Havana, 19 October 1762.[28]

126

A spate of correspondence ensued. Messengers trotted back and forth between the protagonists' houses almost every day. It looks very much as though Don Pedro was enjoying himself. On 22 October he sent the following letter to Albemarle:

> Your Excellency: Yesterday afternoon, between four and five o'clock, I was visited on behalf of Your Excellency by a person, of whose christian name, surname and nationality I am ignorant. I only know that he speaks Spanish with a foreigner's bad pronunciation, and that he wears little gold rings in his ears as women do. I noted that in our conversation he addressed me as *usted*. I informed him of the respectful manner with which he should treat me. He replied that he would always address me in the *usted* form. I assume that this stubbornness indicates that his rank allows him exceptional treatment. I asked him if this was so, and he replied that the only privilege he enjoyed was that of firing cannonballs on behalf of his King. He continued upon this theme at some length, and bade me farewell in a loud voice, and because his demeanour demonstrated a lack of respect for my dignity and it is appropriate that he be corrected, I depend on Your Excellency's fulfilling this duty.[29]

Since Albemarle's demand for a 'donation' from the church had not been met, it is not surprising that this letter brought the bishop no satisfaction. Matters came to a head at the end of October. Among the articles of Havana's capitulation had been the stipulation that the Catholic faith could be maintained in Cuba only on condition that ecclesiastical preferments were sanctioned by Albemarle. The commander had repeatedly requested a list of the priests in the diocese from the bishop, who applied all manner of diversionary tactics to avoid supplying it. Albemarle had reached the end of his tether. On 29 October he told Don Pedro that if he continued in his refusal to cooperate he would have to suffer the consequences and that his, Albemarle's, time was far too precious to dispute over trifles.

Eventually, on 3 November 1762, Albemarle signed an order for Don Pedro's expulsion. It accused him of sedition, and Albemarle declared that if the city was to know any peace at all, it was absolutely necessary that the pestilent prelate be removed. Don Pedro's response to the order was that in matters spiritual he recognized no one but the Holy Father, and in matters temporal no one but the king of Spain, but that his 'miserable body' was 'at the disposition of the heretics'.[30] When he heard these martyrish remarks Albemarle was all for doing the thing properly and hanging Don Pedro, but his colleagues persuaded him of the lack of wisdom of this course. Instead, Don Pedro was hustled onto the next boat to Florida, at six o'clock in the morning on 13 November, without any breakfast. Defiant to the end, he refused to walk to the boat. Sitting on his throne, and wearing his robes, his ring and his crucifix, he had to be carried to the wharf by four British sailors.

Just over three months later, on 10 February 1763, a peace treaty was signed in Paris by France, Spain and England. Havana was returned to the Spanish in exchange for Florida, despite the assertion by William Pitt the Elder, who argued against the treaty, that from the moment of Havana's capture 'all the riches and treasures of the Indies lay at our feet'.[31]

Don Pedro Morell de Santa Cruz returned to Havana, but he was not to live much longer. He received the last rites on a stormy October day in 1768, clung to life for weeks with the same obstinacy that had so enraged Lord Albemarle and finally died that December.

On 6 July 1763, the last of the British forces departed from the city. On the morning of the following day Don Ambrosio Funes de Villapando, Conde de Ricla, entered Havana amid great pomp and jubilation and processed down Calle Muralla to the Plaza Vieja. There an ancient plaque on the wall, 'in memory of the Excelentísimo Señor', stands as a reminder that Muralla used to be called Calle Ricla in the Conde's honour.

The first priorities of the returning Spaniards were the repair of the forts damaged by the British and the construction of new ones in the areas that had been shown during the siege to be of strategic importance. Between 1764 and 1774 an enormous fortress was constructed on the Cabaña hill. Named San Carlos de la Cabaña in honour of Carlos III, it was not only the largest fort in the Americas but also staggeringly expensive: its construction cost over 14 million pesos.

It had been intelligent of the Habaneros to name the fortress after the king, as this may have gone some way towards placating him in the face of such a horrendous sum. Rumour has it that when he heard that the fort had finally been completed he requested a telescope, remarking that considering how much the building had cost, it should certainly be large enough to see from Madrid.

The Fortaleza de San Carlos de la Cabaña stretches along the eastern side of the harbour entrance. Its construction was supervised by the military engineer Silvestre Abarca as part of his extensive plan for 'The Defence of Havana and her Castles'. Along the massive walls of the Cabaña stand enormous cannon with lyrical names like *La Hermosa* (*The Handsome*) and

La Fuerte (*The Strong*). A *cañonazo* is still fired from the Cabaña every night at nine o'clock. This used to be the signal for the closing of the city gates and the raising of the chain to seal the harbour mouth. Although both the gates and the chain are long gone, the gun's shattering roar rushes one back to the dark and fearful nights of Havana in the eighteenth century.

Silvestre Abarca's plan also recommended the construction of the Castillo del Príncipe (at the western end of the Avenida Salvador Allende) and the Castillo de Santo Domingo de Atarés (on the Loma de Soto, to the southwest of the bay). The Príncipe (Prince) was named in honour of Carlos III's son. It was built between 1767 and 1779 in the form of an irregular pentagon. The Atarés was named in honour of the new governor's father, the Conde de Atarés. It was begun in 1763 and completed four years later. Both castles were constructed under the direction of the Belgian engineer, Auguste Cramer.

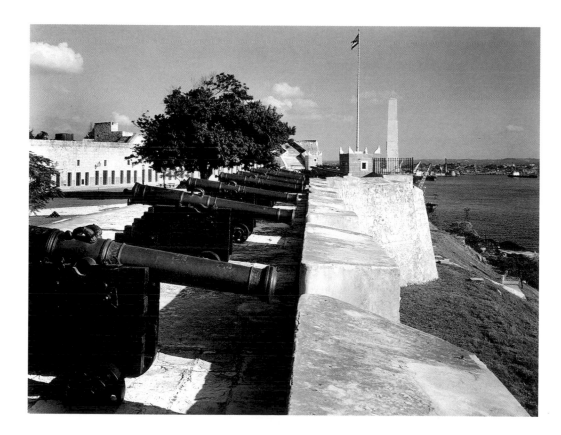

Above: The Fortaleza de San Carlos de la Cabaña and the bay of Havana.

Overleaf left: The chapel of the Fortaleza de San Carlos de la Cabaña.

Overleaf right: Inside the Fortaleza de San Carlos de la Cabaña.

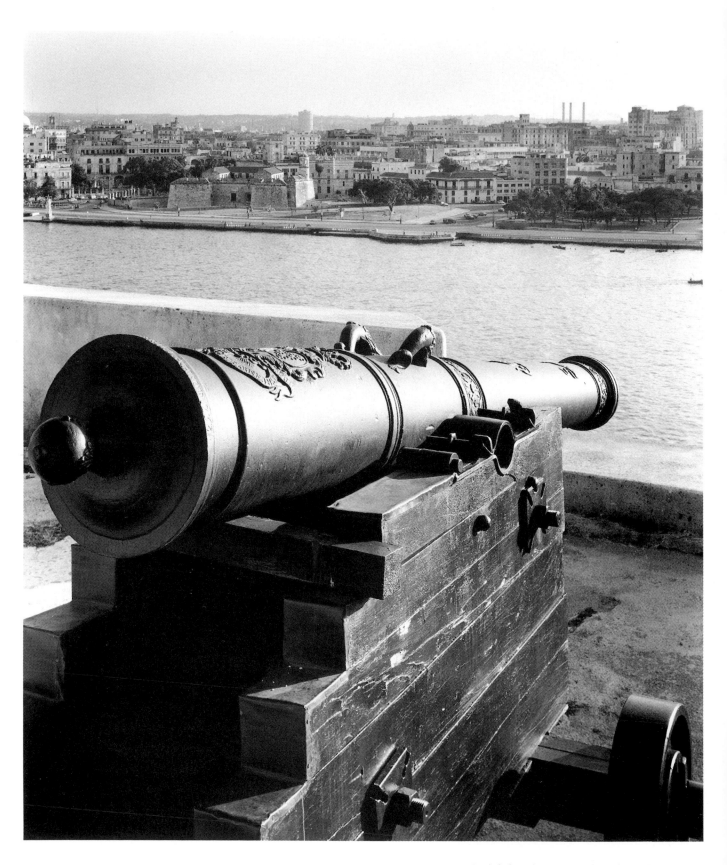

A nightly salute is still fired from the Cabaña.

In terms of Havana's development the English invasion had been a necessary evil. Although so much life and prestige had been lost, and so much damage had been done, the importance that had been attached to the campaign had finally established Havana's tremendous value in the eyes of the Spanish crown and demonstrated the necessity of paying it the attention it deserved. The brief occupation of the city initiated an economic boom that was to enable the construction of some of the city's finest buildings. The scene was set for the theatrical brilliance of the nineteenth century. The cast was waiting in the wings.

'A View of the Market Place in the City of the Havana'.

134

7
SLAVERY

When I think on the course I have run,
From my childhood itself to this day,
I tremble, and fain would I shun,
The remembrance its terrors array.

I marvel at struggles endured,
With a destiny frightful as mine,
At the strength for such efforts: – assured
Tho' I am, 'tis in vain to repine.

I have known this sad life thirty years,
And to me, thirty years it has been
Of suff'ring, of sorrow and tears,
Ev'ry day of its bondage I've seen.

But 'tis nothing the past – or the pains,
Hitherto I have struggled to bear,
When I think, oh my God! on the chains,
That I know I'm yet destined to wear.

Juan Francisco Manzano[1]

EHIND THE SCENES IN the city there was a mass of humanity whose voices were seldom heard. Havana's development had brought it growing fame as an international slave market. Negroes had been first brought to Cuba by the early settlers. They worked alongside the Indians to extract gold from the rivers for the Spanish. The extermination of Cuba's Indian population prompted further imports of slaves from Africa. The Indians had been inconveniently delicate and it was thought that, with their robust physique, the Africans would surely prove to be a more durable option for the performance of the hard manual labour that had hastened the Indians' demise.

In the sixteenth century skilled slaves were valuable property. On 22 January 1579, when Jerónimo de Rojas y Avellaneda sold three Africans to a fellow Habanero, the details of the transaction were meticulously noted:

> Bill of sale given by Jerónimo de Rojas y Avellaneda, citizen of Havana, in favour of Domingo Pereira, also citizen of this town… three slaves, named Antón (metal worker) of the Cape nation, of about thirty-five years, Francisco (sailor), of over forty years, of the Carabalí nation, and Antonio… of over fifty years, for 1,200 ducados, being the price at which the value of the property is estimated.[2]

The customary disclaimer was added to the document:

> If the said slaves of the above names prove to be thieves, or drunkards, or to be lame, or if they prove to have had or to have any infirmity, either all of them or any one of them, the terms of sale will still apply, and if all of them or any one of them prove to have any defects, the terms of sale will still apply for they have been inspected, and there will thus be no future recourse or remedy for reclamation of the payment.[2]

The sixteenth-century Spanish in Havana had already developed cruelty to their slaves into an art. When an African had the temerity to run away, he would be hunted by dogs and mounted men and brought back to the city. There horrific tortures awaited him. After the first attempted escape the authorities contented themselves with administering a flogging. However, should the slave be so ill-advised as to run away again one of his ears would be sliced off. After the third attempt he would lose his other ear. Many runaway slaves killed themselves rather than be taken.

Cuba had one of the lowest slave populations in the Caribbean until the last decades of the eighteenth century, when the demand soared. The British played a major part in the increase of Cuban slavery. Lord Albemarle initiated the trend by selling off about 1,200 slaves whom he had purchased for use in the taking of Havana, and despite later Spanish attempts to retain a monopoly many British slave merchants established themselves in the city. The Habaneros themselves began to make enormous fortunes out of the Africans, either directly as slave merchants or indirectly through the vast profits realized by the sale of sugar. The slaves had to do all the back-breaking work of cutting and processing the cane. During the harvest they worked for sixteen hours every day, with only the briefest pauses for food. Their owners owed their mansions and their exquisite furnishings, their silks, satins and jewels, their carriages and all their pretty little toys and luxuries to the agony of fellow human beings regarded as beasts of burden, base and primitive, without spiritual needs.

In nineteenth-century Cuba the slaves were not encouraged to have children – pregnant women, while being unable to tackle strenuous tasks, cost money to feed. Anyway, supplies had become plentiful and cheap. When a black died of overwork and exhaustion one simply bought a new one. Many Cuban slaves refused as a matter of principle to let cane sugar, the product that perpetuated their misery, pass their lips. Leon Beauvallet, a European visitor to

Havana in 1856, wrote 'Your beet root is a rampant abolitionist! And you will see, one day the slave race will set up statues to it.'³

Thousands of bewildered Africans arrived in Havana every year to begin their life sentence to white whim. On the long voyages to Cuba they were scientifically packed into the ships so as not to waste a particle of space or potential profit. Chained together, seasick and starving by turns, they wallowed in their own filth in dark and airless misery. 'The painful compression of the wretched negroes, in the holds of these vessels, during their voyage across the Atlantic, is too horrible to be described,' wrote the Englishman Joseph John Gurney in 1840, 'Surely this traffic is the most odious wickedness that ever disgraced or afflicted mankind!'⁴ If too many of his cargo died, a slaver would often make a piratical attack on a colleague to replenish his depleted stocks before sailing into the port.

After being unloaded, the Africans were marched off to barracoons, where they were stored until they could be sold. The barracoons in Havana were deliberately sited in one of the most popular recreational areas of the city, at the western end of the Paseo (now Avenida Salvador Allende) near the pleasure-gardens of the governor's summer palace. Passers-by were thus able to view the goods, saving the slavers some of the expense of advertising. The railway line into Havana from the country passed close by the spot, and travellers used to lean from the windows and exchange laughing remarks at the quaintness of the Negroes who, terrified at the passing of the train, would scream and poke their arms and legs through the bars of their communal cage in a most diverting fashion. Visitors to the city used to take afternoon drives up the Paseo to view the savages. Sometimes the barracoons were filled with newly imported black children, so thin that their bones seemed to be about to pierce their skin, their twig-like limbs covered with cuts and grazes from being roughly crammed into the holds of the ships.

Before long notices of sale were placed in the newspapers. The buyers arrived on the appointed day and crowded into the waiting room. From behind a massive door in front of them, blocked by a row of burly guards, came despairing wails and the sound of fists beating against the wooden panels. Heat and tension rose, for by no means all of the slave sales in Havana were conducted as orderly auctions. At a given signal the doors would be flung open and a scene of total mayhem ensued. The buyers rushed in and fell on the naked blacks, indiscriminately grabbing as many as possible in the hope of ending up with a prime

A pretty euphemism for
the horrors of the crossing:
'The Voyage of the Sable Venus,
from Angola to the West Indies'.

The barbaric reality of
loading a slave ship.

specimen. Sometimes one African would be seized by both arms at once by two different buyers, and a furious argument followed, while the moaning victim was pulled back and forth between the prospective purchasers. Some of the slaves would be knocked down and trampled on in the mêlée. These were usually the women who, placed just inside the door on the assumption that they would thus be more clearly seen, bore the brunt of the buyers' mad rush into the room.

Eventually the chaos would quieten a little, and the buyers began to examine their hoard. Every part of the Africans' bodies would be prodded and tweaked, and they were asked a few brisk questions to establish whether or not they understood any Spanish. If they seemed satisfactory, they were given a few articles of clothing and a cigar to calm them down, and were dragged off to be paid for. The weeping and pleadings would then commence in earnest. Nobody paid the slightest attention to whether or not any of their victims had families. Parents, children and siblings were peremptorily separated. Women bought as wet-nurses never saw their babies again.

Once purchased, the Negroes were either dispatched to work on the plantations or taken to grand Havana mansions as house slaves. Here their duties ranged from cooking, valeting and waiting at table to stacking stores in the ground floor warehouse areas, hauling sugar, coffee or tobacco to the port for loading, serving as grooms and messengers and making shoes for the household. Whenever slaves were not needed, if the family went to the country, for instance, their owners would hire them out to their friends and acquaintances. Most houses in Havana were staffed by twenty or thirty slaves, but important figures such as Don Mateo Pedroso y Florencia had a hundred or more. The slaves of Havana's nobility wore liveries decorated with the arms of Cárdenas, or Jaruco, or Pedroso, and took the family's name as their own.

The slave quarters were usually located in the entresols of the houses, conveniently placed for an instant response to the imperious demands of their owners. There was no system of bells. One simply opened one's door and leaned over the balcony rail and yelled for attention. The slaves had to drop everything and run to do their masters' bidding on pain of punishment. Not all the owners were cruel – some slaves became so fond of the families that they served that they refused to work for anyone else – but the majority of masters and mistresses did not treat their Negroes kindly. A few houses in Havana still have iron rings attached to their walls, to which unsatisfactory slaves would be chained to be taught a lesson.

If their owners did not feel equal to punishing them for real or imagined crimes or simply thought they might be getting slack, the slaves were sent to a special whipping place near the Punta, where the onerous task was carried out by trained experts. There was a standard menu of punishments to choose from. It included the *novenario* (nine lashes a day for nine days), the *escalera* (in which the slave was tied to a ladder for flogging), the *boca abajo llevando cuenta* (in which the slave had to lie face down, counting the lashes aloud and if a mistake was made the punishment was repeated from the beginning), and the *boca abajo doble*

Above: Punishing a slave.

Opposite: The entresol of the Casa de Don Mateo Pedroso, in which his slaves were housed.

(for which the slave was tied face down, with alternate lashes being given by two officials at once). Passers-by used to hear agonized screams penetrating the thick walls of the punishment building.

Slaves committed suicide by hanging, eating earth, taking poison or suffocating themselves with their own tongues rather than go through these tortures. The Condesa de Merlín thought the Lucumí people were a particular nuisance in this respect, remarking that they had violent tempers and were inclined to hang themselves at the slightest opposition to their will. The Negroes believed that after their death they would be miraculously returned to Africa.

Many people regarded the slaves, even after they had been dressed in 'civilized' clothing, as dangerous barbarians. An American visiting Havana in 1856 made the stern recommendation that ladies should not on any account walk in the streets for fear of meeting 'blasphemous, odorous and drunken negroes'.[5] 'Nothing eatable is safe from their depredations,' warned Amelia Murray, who visited the city in the same year, 'and this is not from hunger, for they are always plentifully fed, but from their monkey-like habits.'[6]

The slaves in Cuba did, however, have the legal right to buy their freedom. Many of them dreamed of it day and night. Some saved every penny they had to achieve this goal. Others spent all their money on the lottery in the hope of making up the required sum in one fell swoop. They hardly ever won, and as their hopes were dashed again and again they often took to stealing cash for one last try. They were usually caught and always punished.

Free Negro men worked as artisans or set up small businesses. The women usually hired themselves out in a domestic capacity. Samuel Hazard, another unforgiving visitor to Havana, found the concept of the blacks' freedom repulsive. 'Did you ever see anything more disgusting than that great negro wench,' he wrote in 1873, 'a large clothes basket on her head, a colossal cigar sticking out from between her thick lips, while she walks along, majestically trailing an ill-fitting, loose dress (probably the only article of apparel she has on) after her slipshod strides? She is free, too; and, as many others of them do, puts on airs.'[7]

In the Palacio de Bellas Artes in Havana hang a number of representations of Negroes by Victor Patricio Landaluze, a highly reactionary nineteenth-century painter and political caricaturist. They are an indication of how the Africans were regarded at the time. Landaluze specialized in pictures of black people attempting to imitate white habits, in which the subjects are made to look just enough like monkeys to render them ridiculous. One picture shows a slave who, while doing the dusting, has become enamoured of a white marble bust of a pretty white girl with ringlets and barely concealed breasts. In the partner to that painting, entitled 'In Their Absence', a slave girl has abandoned the sweeping to raid her mistress's wardrobe. She is parading about in an idiotic assortment of clothing, while the portrait of the master of the house looks on approvingly from the wall.

Many white men sacrificed fastidiousness to convenience and took black mistresses, and the half-breed fruits of these unions were usually given their freedom by their generous fathers. Havana's free mulattas became famous in North America and Europe as tempting tidbits for discerning males, for whom these gorgeous women combined the hauteur and passion of Spain with African grace and exoticism. The policy, however, was definitely love them and leave them. Any mulatta who got ideas above her station was apt to come to a sticky end, as did the beautiful Cecilia Valdés, in Cirilo Villaverde's celebrated novel of the same name, who cherished the idea of being accepted into Havana's upper social stratum.

The fate of the mulatta is graphically recorded in a series of nineteenth-century cigarette labels, now held in a collection in Havana's Biblioteca Nacional. Many of the images in the collection are devoted to assessments of female virtues and physical charms, and they are saturated with visual and verbal innuendo. The *Vida y Muerte de la Mulata* depicts a Cuban Harlot's Progress. The series begins with the seduction of a black woman by a middle-class Spanish gentleman with the comment 'He who sows will reap'. In the next image the woman is shown pregnant, defiantly returning her lover's disapproving stare, over the title 'Unwanted Harvest'. She is left alone to raise her pretty daughter, who is considered 'Very Promising' by the gentlemen of the neighbourhood. The little mulatta swiftly grows into a luscious woman and receives her first white lover. She goes from strength to strength, cutting a swathe through an adoring male following, but eventually falls from her pedestal. She hits the bottle and the streets, and is arrested for soliciting. Marched off to gaol, she quickly proceeds to the hospital, suffering, presumably, from something venereal, 'The Consequences', and the last label in the series depicts a grim scene of the municipal hearse, drawn by a mule – 'The End of all Pleasure'.

The celebrated mulattas were picked up by men and showered with compliments and presents, but if they became too demanding they were flicked aside like old cigar butts.

143

'If you love me, you'll be happy'

'We're pretty. That's why they follow us'

'The Punishment'

Images from *Vida y Muerte de la Mulata*
(Life and Death of the Mulatta),
a series of nineteenth-century cigarette labels.

Three cheers for the mulatta in Antonio de las Barras y Prado's frightful poem! One can almost hear her dusting off her palms as she stalks away.

> The mulatta is the fatal apple
> That brought discord to the world.
> New Helen, war accompanies her,
> Every man a Paris, every house a Troy.
>
> Circassian grace shines in her face,
> African light glows from her skin
> And her Norman blood smoulders
> In the hot veins of Ethiopia.
>
> When, to the lugubrious sound of the bell
> Her victim is laid in his grave,
> The cruel mulatta lights her cigar
> And goes to immolate another man at her pleasure.[8]

In 1840 a fascinating book was published in London. It told the story of a Cuban slave, Juan Francisco Manzano, who against all odds had taught himself to read. The volume included a selection of poems that he had written before buying his freedom at the age of thirty-eight.

Juan Francisco was born into slavery. His mistress had mansions both in Havana and in Matanzas, the next large town down the coast. She was a cruel and capricious woman, who alternately fawned upon the little boy and subjected him to horrifying punishments for supposed transgressions. 'I was like my mistress's lap-dog,' he recalled. 'It was my duty to follow her wherever she went.'[9] She dressed him in rich livery covered with gold lace, and he would accompany her to the theatre and to public balls. After being at her beck and call all night the child would become terribly tired. On the drive home he was expected to ride on the back of her carriage and keep the lantern alight. If he fell asleep he was locked into the stocks on arrival at the house in Calle Inquisidor.

Juan was not permitted to relax when his mistress left Havana for her large residence in Matanzas. If he did not respond on the instant to her call he would be shut up in the charcoal shed after nightfall, without food or water in the rat-infested darkness. Often he would imagine that evil spirits were creeping up on him and would let out shrieks of terror,

Slaves in the stocks.

whereupon he would be dragged out, beaten soundly and thrown back into the shed. In middle age Juan Francisco could well remember the terrors and tortures of his youth: 'I led a life of so much misery, daily receiving blows on the face, that often made the blood spout from both my nostrils; no sooner would I hear myself called than I would begin to shiver so that I could hardly keep on my legs.'[10]

Finally, Juan Francisco went to work for an acquaintance of his mistress's. His new master showed him a great deal more kindness. In this happier atmosphere Juan resolved to improve himself. He collected together some pieces of paper and writing tools and employed his spare time in learning the alphabet, tracing the letters from his master's discarded correspondence. One day he was found labouring at this task. His master was not angry, but 'only advised me to drop that pastime, as not adapted to my situation in life, and that it would be more useful to me to employ my time in needle-work'.[11]

The respite was short-lived, for Juan Francisco's first owner suddenly decided that she wanted him back. After a brief period of doting affection she again began to subject him to constant criticism, threats and tortures. He was now quite old enough to be punished by her estate overseer, and when he was falsely accused of stealing a chicken this brutal man 'tied my hands behind me as a criminal, mounted his horse, and commanded me to run quick before him.... Scarcely had I run a mile before the horse, stumbling at every step, when two dogs that were following us, fell upon me; one taking hold of the left side of my face pierced it through, and the other lacerated my left thigh and leg.'[12] The punishment was completed by whippings on nine consecutive nights.

By this time Juan Francisco had taken to writing poetry in secret. One day his mistress ordered him to go with her into the garden to transplant some seedlings.

At the time of leaving the garden, I took unconsciously, a small leaf, one alone of geranium, thinking only of making verses; I was following, with this little leaf in my hand, two or three yards behind my mistress, so absent in my mind that I was squeezing the leaf with my fingers to give it greater fragrancy. At the entrance of the anti-chamber she turned back, I made room for her, but the smell attracted her attention; full of anger, on a sudden and in a quick tone she asked me 'What have you got in your hands?' Motionless and trembling, I dropt the remains of the leaf, and, as if it was a whole plant, for this crime I was struck on the face, and delivered to the care of the overseer, Don Lucas Rodríguez.[13]

Juan Francisco spent the night in the stocks, and at dawn he was given a flogging. 'When my mistress rose next morning, her first care was to inquire whether I was treated as I deserved ... and she asked, if I would dare to take any more leaves of her geranium?'[13]

When Juan Francisco's mother died she left him some money which enabled him to purchase his freedom. He worked successively as a tailor, a hired servant and a house painter. He then set himself up as a confectioner, but the business failed and he lost all his money. When the book *Poems by a Slave in the Island of Cuba* was published he was working as a chef for whoever would hire him.

Throughout Cuba's history there were numerous uprisings among the slaves. In 1812 José Antonio Aponte, a free Negro carpenter who lived in Havana, organized the first national conspiracy. News of the movement spread all over the island via a widely spread network of sympathizers, causing unrest in many cities and plantations. Aponte, the 'Cuban Spartacus', was also a priest of the African Santería religion. His colleagues would meet at his house to progress the plot while pretending to be attending a *misa* (mass) for Changó, Aponte's guiding African spirit. Finally the movement was betrayed and its leaders were executed. Aponte's head was displayed outside his house as a ghastly warning to anyone else who might be nursing plans for the overthrow of slavery.

Despite Spain's agreement of 1817 with the British to abolish it, slaving continued almost to the end of the nineteenth century. Cuba was the last Caribbean island to abolish it. Many of Havana's citizens could not resist the enormous profits to be made in the trade. The city officials, from the governor down to the harbourmaster, raked in vast sums in bribes to ensure their ignorance of what was going on. Opinions vary on how much each *bulto* (package, a euphemism for a newly landed slave) made the governor and his henchmen, but Juan Manzano's patron Dr R. R. Madden estimated that Governor Tacón received £100,000 for exercising his blind eye.

After the Anglo-Spanish agreement had been signed, the British sent representatives to Havana to ensure that the Spanish complied with its terms. They might as well have tried to catch mercury in a sieve as prevent the departure of the swift slaving ships from Havana. When Joseph John Gurney visited the city in April 1840 there were five slavers in the harbour waiting for a dark night to slip past the British and set sail for Africa. These included the *Socorro* (capacity 1,000), the *Grandes Antillas* (capacity 1,200) and the *Duquesa de Braganza*, which had recently collected 1,100 slaves on the African coast, had lost 240 on the middle passage and finally landed 860.

Formal complaints bore no fruit. The trade continued almost under the noses of the British, with cargoes being landed along the coast. When questioned, the slavers arriving in the port would reply with an injured air that they had returned from their voyages in ballast. Whenever the British became too vociferous they would be handed the dregs of a shipment (the old and infirm) who the Spaniards would claim were poor Negroes seized from wicked slavers by virtuous Spanish vessels.

In 1835 the Spanish signed another treaty with the British, which stated that any ship carrying slaving equipment could be seized. It proved of little more use than the 'abolition'. The Spanish slaving ships fell back on the solution of sailing under foreign flags, and the British were unable to accost more than a fraction of the 1,500 to 2,000 vessels that were by then departing annually from Havana.

Gurney estimated that 50,000 slaves were being imported every year in the mid-nineteenth century, and since the profits amounted to between 100 and 200 per cent nobody worried about the loss of part of their shipments. If they were surprised by the British they simply tossed the incriminating evidence overboard. One could not allow the pursuit of profit to become clouded by moral considerations. R. R. Madden broke into impassioned verse to express his condemnation of *The Slave-Trade Merchant*:

Behold, his House! – if marble speak elsewhere,
'Sermons in stones' are with a vengeance here,
Whate'er the potent will of wealth can do
Or pride can wish, is offered to your view.
Those gay saloons, this banquet hall's array,
This glaring pile in all its pomp survey,
The grandeur strikes – one must not look for taste –
What's gorgeous, cannot always be quite chaste.

What cares the merchant for that crowded hold,
The voyage pays, if half the slaves are sold!

'Branding a Negress'.

He need not leave his counting-house, 'tis true,
Nor bid Havana and its joys adieu,
To start the hunt on Afric's burning shore,
And drench its soil with streams of human gore;
He need not part with friends and comrades here
To sever nature's dearest ties elsewhere.[14]

'Inspection and Sale
of a Negro'.

In 1840 an English abolitionist, David Turnbull, was sent to Havana as British consul. He proposed that a census of slaves be taken to establish how many had arrived in Cuba since 1820, all of whom should subsequently be freed. The Spanish would not cooperate. They declared that any increase in numbers since the first treaty was due to breeding. Turnbull continued to press his point, to the extent that Britain and Spain almost went to war and finally, when he tried to organize a slave uprising, Turnbull was expelled from Cuba.

Slavery was eventually abolished in the island in 1888, not so much as a consequence of political pressure as of a crisis in the sugar industry caused mainly by a rapid increase in the production of European beet sugar.

Despite the bitter memories associated with the trade, slavery bequeathed to the island of Cuba a potent cultural legacy, and the African tribal religions are still a deeply felt force in the lives of many Cubans. In order to retain some sense of their identity within a system designed to repress it, the slaves drew on the spiritual resources of their ancient beliefs. They formed *cabildos*, groups defined according to tribal origin, which held frequent meetings all over Havana. Every year on 6 January the Spanish indulged their Negroes by permitting a celebration of their ancestral origins. On the sacred *Día de los Reyes* the Africans would assemble, dressed in the images of their gods, and dance down Calle Oficios to the deep pulse of the bass drums and the sharp rattle of gourds and sticks. Fringed costumes thrashed and whirled, flaming torches swung through the air, high-pitched chants shrilled up and down the street and sweets rained down on the dancers from the balconies. When it reached the Plaza de Armas the crowd streamed through the great doors of the governor's palace. The noise and pandemonium was multiplied into an unimaginable uproar in the stony courtyard, but gradually the voices of the drums sank to a murmur as the leaders of each group solemnly mounted the stairs to receive gifts of money and cigars.

Belief in the powers of the African gods is still celebrated in Cuba today. Devotees of the Abakuá religion of the Carabalí tribe (from part of Nigeria and Cameroon) continue to practise all-male rituals during which the dancers represent 'little devils', the spirits of the dead. The sacred drums of the Abakuá, unlike those of other Afro-Cuban religious sects, are not played; they precede the participants in the rituals, borne ceremonially to the gatherings by chosen individuals. The names of the principal drums are Eribó, Empegó, Ekueñon and

151

Enkrikamo, but the most important drum is the Ekue, which contains the secrets of the power of the Abakuá. The exclusion of women from the Abakuá sect may have something to do with the legend concerning the creation of the first Ekue. The Princess Sikan was fetching water from a river that ran between the territories of two African tribes. By mistake she caught a fish whose name was Tanze and who happened to be a god. Unfortunately for the princess, Tanze died, and the two tribes lost no time in executing Sikan and using her skin to make the first Ekue.

Palo Monte, the religion of the Bantu from around the River Congo, has markedly sinister overtones; some of its rituals are grisly. It centres around the worship of the forces of nature, both good and evil, that are concentrated in the huge cauldron called the Nganga, which is kept in the houses of the savants. When the owner of the Nganga is not at home, it is guarded by the Muñeca de Talanquera, a doll that is chained to its chair so that it cannot run away. The essence of Palo Monte magic is contained in the Mpaka, an animal horn with a mirror fixed in one end. During ceremonies, the mirror is held over a candle flame and the resulting smoke patterns are interpreted by the savants.

Palo Monte has much to do with black magic. If its devotees wish to affect somebody's destiny, they must obtain some of the hair, nail clippings, fragments of clothing and skin of the victim (this last ingredient might be hard to procure without the victim realizing what is happening!) and use it all to stuff a doll made in the image of the victim. If they wish the person to die, they place the doll in a little coffin. If they want the victim to keep a secret, they bind the mouth of the doll. If they want to unite a couple, they tie two dolls face to face. To part a couple, the dolls are tied back to back. If a devotee suspects that someone is working a bad magic on him, he consults an expert on a suitable amulet to carry for his own protection.

The Yoruba belief, which originated in the Lucumí region of Nigeria, is perhaps the most fascinating. In order to retain contact with their gods in the face of Catholic pressure, the devotees of Santería assigned Christian alter egos to their bewildering pantheon of orishas (gods or goddesses), all of whom possess their own colours, numbers, symbols, sacrificial animals and medicinal herbs.

Changó, the African god of thunder, lightning and fire, became Santa Bárbara, the patron saint of the artillery and the foundries. Changó's colours are red and white, and his symbols

A lock in the form of a slave
at the Casa de los Condes de Jaruco.

Above: The Yoruba god Changó,
associated with the Christian Santa Bárbara.

Right: Our Lady of Regla, whose
Yoruba identity is Yemayá.

are a double-headed axe, a sword, a cup and a castle. Babalú Ayé, the comforter and healer of the sick, is St Lazarus. His symbol is a pair of crutches and his colour is light blue. Unlike the others he is a humble god and appears dressed in rags. Our Lady of Mercy is Obatalá, the African goddess of peace, purity and the colour white. Yemayá, the proud and haughty mother of the sea, timid and treacherous by turns, became associated with Our Lady of Regla, the black madonna adopted by the fishermen who lived at Regla on the eastern side of Havana harbour. Her colour is deep blue; her symbols are boats, anchors, propellers, buoys, the sun and the moon. She is summoned with maracas and has several identities relating to the seashore and the shallows. Olokún Yemayá is the deity of the deeps, hugely powerful and mysterious. She can be seen only in dreams, and her name must be pronounced with care.

The patron saint of Cuba, the Virgin of Caridad del Cobre, is represented by Ochún, the goddess of love and passion. Ochún is beautiful, happy and sexy. She is the mistress of the taste of sweetness, honey and its golden colour, the magical number five and the 'sweet waters' of lakes and rivers. Ochún loves dancing, flirting and telling jokes. Her symbols include rocks from rivers, oars, mirrors and fans made of peacock feathers, for the peacock belongs to her. The man who wants to be loved by a daughter of Ochún must chew cinnamon and drink honey. Women who put five sweets smeared with honey in a bowl under their beds for five days believe they will be blessed with Ochún's irresistible power. She can help you to win a man, keep your own, or take someone else's.

During Santería celebrations the gods are invited to manifest themselves through the santeros and santeras, to the accompanying rhythms of the drums. When the priests and priestesses go into a trance the worshippers believe that their deity has come to bless them with his or her divine power. In many houses in Havana there are altars to the orishas, decorated with their images and symbols, both African and Catholic.

Individual tribal allegiances are still strong in modern Cuba. Through the African-inspired rhythm of the *son*, Nicolás Guillén, the Cuban poet who died in 1989, conjured the shades of slavery and called to the descendants of the Africans for the recognition of a unified mulatto identity with the following verse. To feel the *son*, read it aloud with the Spanish sounds: the *uba* syllables are pronounced 'oobah', *í* is a short, emphatic 'ee' sound, and *ll* sounds the same as y, '*llanto*' being pronounced 'yanto'.

Yoruba soy, lloro en yoruba
lucumí.
Como soy un yoruba en Cuba,
quiero que hasta Cuba suba mi llanto
   yoruba,
que suba el alegre llanto yoruba
que sale de mí.

Yoruba soy,
cantando voy,
llorando estoy,
y cuando no soy yoruba,
soy congo, mandinga, carabalí.

I am a Yoruba, I cry in Yoruba
Lucumí.
As I am a Yoruba in Cuba,
I want my Yoruba lament to rise up to Cuba
and let the joyful Yoruba cry
rise up from me.

I am a Yoruba,
I go singing
I am crying,
and when I am not Yoruba,
I am Congo, Mandinga, or Carabalí.

'Europe supported by Africa and America'.
Europe represented as a guileless and fragile innocent,
willingly sustained by noble savages.

155

8

SOCIETY IN THE NINETEENTH CENTURY

What has thou, Cuban? Life itself resign, –
Thy very grave is insecurely thine!
Thy blood, thy treasure, poured like tropic rain
From tyrant hands to feed the soil of Spain.

José María Heredia[1]

The women look upon the United States as a country to be dreamed of as a fairy vision, where life and liberty are to be really enjoyed, or as one sweet innocent inquired, "Every one is free there now, Señor?"

"Oh, yes," I replied; "we have no negro slaves there now."

"No, no! Señor; you don't understand me. I mean the women, too, – are they not free?"

To which I was compelled to reply they were, and only we poor men were their slaves.

"Es muy bueno, Señor, it is not so here."

Samuel Hazard[2]

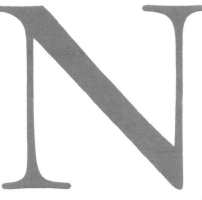

NINETEENTH-century Havana had truly come of age and was celebrating. The city was elegant and sophisticated, exciting and excitable, noisy and witty. Down went the walls – they couldn't contain the energy that the city generated. The streets were full of cafés, bars and casinos. Every day was a vibrant parade, every night a dance, and tourists, visitors and traders came from all over the world to admire and enjoy them. The view of the city was cross-hatched with thousands of masts and spars; the wakes of the cargo boats drew lines of light across the harbour, and an endless stream of luxuries and delicacies was piled into the warehouses: cocoa from Venezuela, indigo from Guatemala, cochineal from Mexico, leaf tobacco, gold, silver, Castile soap, molasses, leather, sugar, wines, spices, coffee, rum, cigars, glassware, silk, wool, linen, Spanish and Dutch brandy.

From well before dawn on a typical day until long after dusk a river of noise and colour coursed through the streets, and swirled more slowly around the squares. Early in the morning crowds of peasants travelled in from the countryside to Havana's markets. Their trains of donkeys, tied nose to tail, carried vast panniers of fruit and vegetables and flapping bunches of live chickens hanging upside-down by their feet. Wooden carts pulled by

The fountain of 'La Noble Habana'.

cream-coloured oxen creaked slowly along. Bundles of hay seemed to be moving down the street independently, until the furry ears and tail of a mule came into view. Farmers strode by with live pigs slung across their shoulders. Cows and goats were driven from door to door and milked straight into the jug. Carriers brought buckets of evil-smelling water from the local fountains to those houses without their own supply, where pieces of sulphur were added to the slimy liquid in an effort to purify it.

The ground floors of the mansions were filled with footsteps and voices, the sounds of horses being saddled and led out from the stables, barrels and bales being swung onto handcarts and trundled off to the docks, and scores of caged birds singing. Monkeys, parrots and slave children ran about in the dust. The fountains in the courtyards splashed the columns with moving darts of light. Upstairs the slaves put out their masters' black frock coats, fine linen shirts and silk cravats. In the kitchen silver trays were laid with freshly baked bread and *café con leche*.

'The Baker and the Hay-Merchant' by Federico Miahle.

As the sun rose higher, straight-backed Dons on shiny thoroughbreds began to pick their way through the crowds, and the volantas were driven into the streets. There were 3,000 of these wonderfully elegant and utterly impractical little carriages in Havana. They had light bodies slung between two enormous wheels, and their long, curved shafts were carried by

one well-groomed horse, ridden by a Negro postilion – known as a *calesero* – in extravagant livery. His scarlet, bottle-green or purple velvet jacket was smothered in gold or silver lace. He wore immaculate white breeches, a white waistcoat and a black silk hat with a gold or silver band. His legs were encased in black leather gaiters, polished to a mirror-finish, and although his feet inside his shiny-buckled shoes were bare, his smooth black ankles looked as if they were encased in black silk stockings. His solid silver stirrups bore his master's coat of arms. He carried a long leather whip.

A volanta. Engraving by James Gay Sawkins.

The volantas, suspended in mid-air between their wheels on thick leather straps, were mercifully very comfortable. The *caleseros* drove them down the streets at a cracking pace, scattering pedestrians and animals to left and right. However, their prodigious length meant that they were almost unable to negotiate the tight corners of Old Havana. 'It is a matter of considerable difficulty,' wrote Samuel Hazard, 'the horse and rider appearing as though they would have to enter some store-door to get out of the way of the volanta behind it, and is the occasion of much hard swearing'.[3] It was impossible for two volantas to pass each other without their wheels becoming inextricably locked, so a one-way system was set up. Some of its signs, a pointing hand in a frilly cuff, are still embedded in the walls.

Above: A corner of Old Havana embellished with an ancient pointing hand and a modern one-way sign.

Opposite: The ground floor of the Casa de los Condes de Jaruco.

The streets are still as narrow as they ever were, and venturing into the maze in a car is not to be undertaken lightly by those of a nervous or impatient disposition. It is the modern one-way system that now occasions the hard swearing. Old Havana, jammed with traffic on a sweltering day, turns sightseers into psychotics. In the nineteenth century, however, impatience was the province of carriage-drivers, slaves and merchants. For the typical gentleman of Havana, descended from an old Spanish family, haste was both unnecessary and unfashionable. He had more time and money on his hands than he knew what to do with. If his estates were being well-managed and his slaves were adequately controlled by his overseers, the only effort left to be made was that of passing the time.

Lying late in his billowy bed he would languidly review the day's possibilities. He might drive to the countryside, spend the afternoon in a café or a bar, try out a horse or buy his mulatta a present. There were hundreds of stores to choose from in the city, but the best ones were in Calles Obispo and O'Reilly. They were stuffed to bursting with china and glass ornaments, candles and incense, jewellery made by the finest European craftsmen and fabrics such as exquisite piña cloth, a silky gauze made of pineapple fibre and dyed in brilliant colours. The name of each shop was written in golden lettering over the door. The titles were whimsical; planets, gods and goddesses, fruits, flowers, heroes, apostles. One could buy muslins and ribbons at St Anthony's, medicines at St Dominic's, tapes and trimmings from The Empress Eugenia or cakes from The Goddess Diana.

The entire lengths of both streets, from the Plaza de Armas to the double Monserrate gate, were covered with coloured awnings, stretched between the buildings to soften the glare of the sun. Beneath them, in the subdued glow of light, filled with teetering piles of shiny novelties and the chatter of bargaining, the streets seemed like oriental bazaars.

The pavements seethed. Vendors displayed trays of needles, pins and buttons. Slaves without pockets carried a cigar behind one ear, a match behind the other, and coins inside both. Raggedy old men, sitting on the ground among their cards and dice, loudly advertised chances for passing gamblers. Acrobats in spangled tights writhed on little squares of carpet. Chinese crockery-sellers in floppy slippers, with heavy baskets hanging from yokes on their shoulders, called customers from their houses with the continuous clatter of a pile of plates juggled with one hand. Beggars, papery bags of bones, whined from the doorways.

His interest fading, the gentleman would consult his fat gold watch with a sigh. Perhaps he might visit the circus and take a stroll around the booths displaying foreign curiosities: the American Monster Horse, the Incredible Monkey Boy, the Erudite Pig From London. Or perhaps he would go to a bullfight... it was amusing when they stuck the firework darts into the bulls to make them run. But if he required real excitement, something to lighten the endless dullness of the day, he would hail a volanta and instruct the driver to take him to the Valla de Gallos.

The cockfights in Havana were held in covered pits where seats were ranged around a small circular arena. Slaves, free Negroes, poor whites and gentlemen crowded into the tiny spaces for the fights, which took place in an atmosphere of cacophonous frenzy. The scrawny, balding cockerels were matched *al cotejo*, according to the length of their natural spurs, or *al peso*, by weight, and they often fought *de cuchilla*, when their owners tied artificial spurs to their charges' legs for a more flamboyantly bloody display. After being teased into a

'Valla de Gallos' by Federico Miahle.

rage, the cockerels were released into the ring where they flew ferociously at each other, pecking, stabbing and clawing. The spectators went wild, stamping their feet, fighting each other for a better view, roaring, howling and shrieking 'Mata! Mata!' (Kill! Kill!). The air filled with dust, bets were exchanged by a system of hand signals (it was impossible for anything to be heard in the din) and eventually the fight would reach a gruesome conclusion of bloodstained feathers and pecked-out eyes. The victor was parted from his opponent and wiped down. His owner squirted a mouthful of *aguardiente* (rum) over his head to clean his wounds and blew a little alum into his eyes through a straw to staunch the bleeding.

Many Habaneros adored a cockfight, but when taken to the pits for a treat, the fastidious foreigners were horrified. 'If you want to see the workings of all the evil passions in the human face,' remarked Samuel Hazard, 'just pay one visit to a cock-fight, and I'll guarantee you'll not go again, but will come away intensely disgusted.'[4]

In the evening, if he were not worn out by the day's exertions, the gentleman might visit the theatre. Havana's citizens were great opera enthusiasts. Behind its somewhat dismal Doric exterior, the new Teatro Tacón was an airy confection of white and gold latticework, and its enormous central chandelier held 1,000 lights. The theatre had cost $2,000,000 to build, and in its heyday it had 600 weapons in its stage armoury and almost 14,000 costumes. When one of the internationally famous singers and actresses appearing at the Tacón excelled herself, the Habaneros rose to their feet and pelted her with flowers, balloons trailing streamers of coloured ribbon, purses of gold, diamond jewellery and white doves with love poems attached to their legs.

After the theatre, the gentleman might repair to a casino. Gambling was dear to the hearts of the Habaneros. They would sit over the cards and dice until the early hours, in plushy gaming houses where the gas lamps were reflected a thousand times in the mirrors, and starving beggars clustered around the door, lying in wait for reckless winners. Crime had ridden hard on the heels of wealth into Havana. Regla, the little town across the bay, developed into a rendezvous for smugglers. They would often be joined by gentlemen looking for thrills. Most people knew what was afoot, but the Spanish were unable to put a stop to it.

Shanty towns had sprung up on the outskirts of the city, where freed slaves, beggars and cripples lived in conditions of unimaginable squalor. The areas became more cut-throat as deserters from the rigid discipline of the Spanish army gravitated towards them. These desperadoes would go to any extreme of murder or robbery in order to survive. If they took up conventional employment they were bound to be caught and taken to face the inevitable public death by firing squad.

> The order was given; the bright morning sun shone like living fire along the polished barrels of the guns, as the fatal muzzles all ranged in point at the heart of the condemned. 'Fuego!' (fire) said the commanding officer. A report followed, accompanied by a cloud of smoke, which the sea breeze soon dispersed, showing us the still upright form of the victim. Though wounded in many places, no vital part was touched, nor did he fall until his sergeant, advancing quickly, with a single reserved shot blew his brains over the surrounding greensward.[5]

Some of the entrepreneurial initiatives adopted by the inhabitants of the shanty towns were horribly creative. Shoppers in Havana's markets were delighted when a novel delicacy suddenly appeared on the stalls: a previously unknown type of charcuterie called the French sausage. Everyone in the city was eating it and pronouncing it quite the most delicious thing they had ever tasted. One day a particular lady sent her slave to the market to buy some. Hours passed, the señora's mouth watered, but the girl did not return. In a great rage, her mistress instructed the authorities to find and punish her runaway slave. They found her but she was past punishing: most of her was already on sale in the Plaza Vieja. All that was left was her head, on top of an enormous heap of bodies in the French sausage factory, two miles outside the Monserrate gate.

The sausage-manufacturers turned out to be a gang of about fifty Spanish, Portuguese, French and Italian thugs who prowled Havana selecting plump Negroes for the mincer. They were rounded up and clapped into cells in the Morro. Twelve of them were hanged and the rest were sent to work in Spanish mines, but the boss of the gang managed to bribe his way to freedom.

Another dubious character who answered a commercial challenge with creative flair was Don Francisco Marty y Torrens. During the 1830s Governor Miguel Tacón y Rosíque was struggling to suppress the activities of the smugglers, with a notable lack of success. Finally he hit upon the idea of offering a substantial reward to any smuggler who would desert the fraternity and apply his inside knowledge to catching his ex-colleagues. A further sum was offered if the notorious leader of the smugglers, Francisco Marty, could be brought to justice. One night, several months after the offer had been broadcast, Tacón was sitting at his desk upstairs in the Palacio de los Capitanes Generales. Suddenly a mysterious cloaked stranger opened the door of the governor's inner sanctum and slipped into the room. Tacón was about to summon the guard who had so incompetently failed to prevent the intrusion, but his ears pricked up when the man began to talk about smuggling and ask pointed questions about the rewards on offer. A long, exasperating conversation followed, during which the stranger repeatedly asked whether the reward would be accompanied by a pardon. Finally, just as Tacón was about to have him arrested, the man revealed that he was none other than the infamous Pancho Marty.

A deal was struck. The governor equipped Marty with boats and men and sent him forth to clean up Havana. A number of raids were carried out, but the criminals often vanished mysteriously with their stores before the troops could reach them. However, Governor Tacón seemed satisfied and offered the reward to the reformed smuggler. To his surprise it was refused, but Marty made him a proposition. He asked for the monopoly on all the sales of fish in the city, in return for which he undertook to build a large stone fish market on Calle Empedrado, which would revert to the government after a few years. Tacón considered the proposal to be most acceptable; anything to avoid actual expenditure. He consented, and Marty swiftly became one of Havana's wealthiest citizens. When he gave up the fish market he struck a similar bargain over theatrical productions, building the celebrated Teatro Tacón. He managed it with singular entrepreneurial skill, to a chorus of resentful noises off from underpaid thespians.

By the middle of the nineteenth century 44,000 people were living within the confines of Old Havana. The interiors of the eighteenth-century mansions were fitted out in the latest style with every luxury that money could buy. The exteriors were covered in ornament, from their original baroque stonework to the delicate traceries of their wrought iron balconies and *rejas*. Their walls were painted in every conceivable colour. 'One house has walls of a light green, with pink cornices and mouldings,' wrote a startled American visitor. 'Its neighbour is a delicate blue, with salmon trimmings; the next is gray and orange, with some admixture of white – or lilac and yellow, or pink and blue – all shimmering and quivering in the hot, glowing air'.[6]

The drive leading to the Quinta de los Molinos.

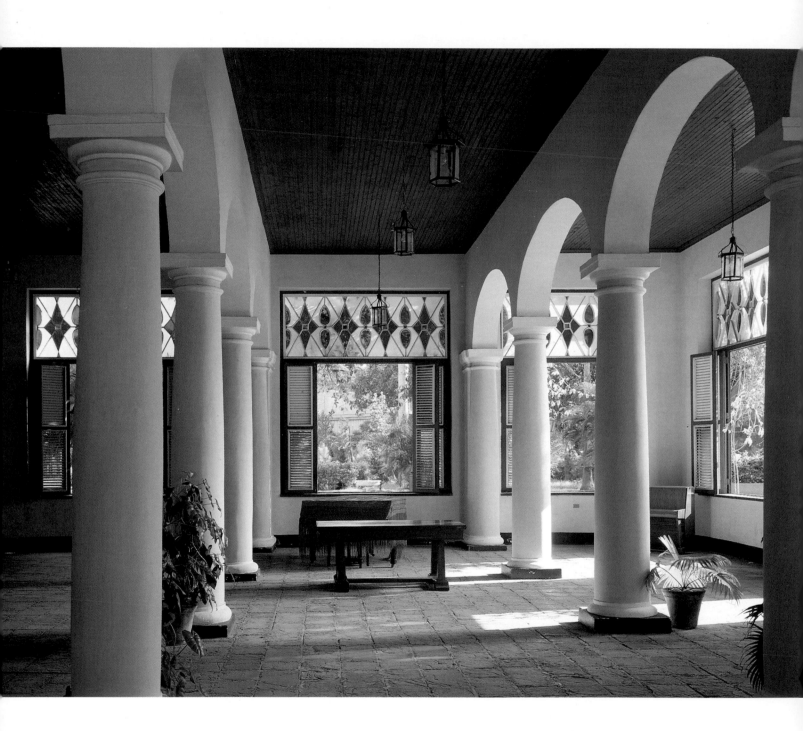

The Quinta de los Molinos.

The streets had by now been given most of the names that they possess today. Calle Empedrado was the first to be cobbled. An enormous avocado tree had grown in Calle Aguacate. Calle Sol had a large sun painted on the side of one of the houses in the street. Calle Tejadillo had been the original location of the first house to boast a tiled roof. The balconies of Calle Damas were thronged with girls. An official of the Inquisition, Don Antonio Claudio de la Luz, had lived in a house in Calle Inquisidor. One of the inhabitants of Calle Lamparilla kept a little lamp burning day and night in honour of the saints.

There was not a square centimetre left *intramuros* for further building. If the staggering wealth of the sugar aristocracy was to be given architectural expression, it would have to take place outside the walls. The completion in 1827 of the Templete, an elegant little Doric temple designed by Coronel Antonio María de la Torre y Cárdenas (on the east side of the Plaza de Armas), set the neoclassical ball rolling through the streets and out of the gates. It was given an extra push by Bishop Juan José Díaz de Espada y Fernández de Landa, who arrived in Havana on 25 February 1802, bursting with new European ideas. He laid out a cemetery outside the walls with a neoclassical gate and chapel. In an excess of modern zeal, he removed the baroque altars of the cathedral, 'which, full of columns, decorations, gilding and mouldings … darken and dominate the places in which the faithful pray',[7] and put neoclassical ones in their place.

The baroque bowed out, and a stony parade of Doric, Ionic and Corinthian columns marched westwards along the graceful boulevards which stretched into the countryside. Governor Tacón had the Paseo laid out from the walls to the Castillo del Príncipe. Many palaces set in extensive grounds were erected along its length, including the governor's own summer residence, the Quinta de los Molinos. Los Molinos were the royal snuff mills, which were located on the site in 1791. This was in order to take advantage of the proximity of the waters of the Zanja Real, which were channelled around the mills to aid the manufacturing process. At the back of the Quinta, a graceful villa set in elegant gardens, a portion of the aqueduct still remains. More *quintas* (grand country houses) began to spring up in the hills of Cerro, to the southwest of the old city. The Quinta de Santovenia, an imposing summer house with inlaid marble floors and ornate wrought iron *rejas*, was littered with fountains and statuary. It has been beautifully preserved by the nuns who run it as an old people's home.

Nineteenth-century house-building was intensely competitive and each new villa was

169

more extravagantly Italianate than the last. Cerro became the place to retire during the torrid months between May and August. The Habaneros would spend the summer poring over their plans for an English-style park and a boating lake with real gondolas, feeding the pet alligator kept in a landscaped pool and chatting the days away in the breezy patio. Here, fragrant flowers, marble benches and pomegranate trees provided Samuel Hazard with 'a charming place in which to dream one's idle hours away or flirt desperately with *las bonitas Señoritas*'.[8]

Statuary had become all the rage. Don Claudio Martínez de Pinillos, Conde de Villa-nueva, presented the city with two sumptuous fountains carved by Giuseppe Gaggini. The Fountain of the Lions, having been moved about all over Havana, now stands in its original site in the Plaza de San Francisco. The Fuente de la India stands just north of the junction of Calle Dragones and the Prado. This fountain is surmounted by a Carrara marble statue of a Junoesque Indian maiden, clad in palm leaves, feathers and fringed drapery, holding a cornucopia in one hand and a shield bearing the arms of Havana in the other. She soon became known as 'La Noble Habana' in honour of the legendary Indian queen after whom the province of Havana was named. The new architectural fashions were expressed not only in the *quintas*. Luxurious urban residences were built near the walls. One of these, which still stands as a monument to its owner's stupendous if fleeting wealth, is the Palacio de Aldama.

Don Domingo de Aldama arrived in Cuba in 1808. He worked his way out of poverty, first as a merchant and later as a sugar planter. His son Miguel continued his success, becoming one of Havana's richest citizens and the owner of an impressive list of sugar mills. His palace was designed by Manuel José Carrerá. It was built facing the Campo de Marte, the military parade ground, which was later to become the Parque de la Fraternidad Americana.

The palace is enormous. Its patio is too tremendously grand to enjoy any of the intimate atmosphere of Havana's earlier aristocratic mansions. Balconies overlook it and doors lead into it from every direction. Its columns are severe; its marble fountain is tall and imposing. No frivolity has been permitted to soften the great staircase, made of massive blocks of marble and dominated by grandiose iron lamps. Even its wrought iron *rejas* are forbiddingly formal. All the decorative elements are ponderous: thick iron grilles, formal Pompeian paintings on the ceilings, heavily decorated tiles, inlaid marble floors. Its owner crammed the spacious rooms with gilded furniture, Persian rugs, vast mirrors, paintings by European

The Quinta de Santovenia.

masters, Gobelin tapestries, heavy chandeliers and Chinese and Japanese bronzes. But de Aldama was not content merely to multiply his fortune and enjoy its trappings. He became embroiled in the complexities of Cuban politics.

The white inhabitants of nineteenth-century Havana were divided into *Criollos* (those born in Cuba) and *Peninsulares* (native Spaniards). The passionate loathing of one group for the other increased with every passing day. The flames were fanned by Governor Tacón, who looked like a particularly unpleasant spider in spectacles, and behaved like a martinet. His brisk programme of urban reform (to include street cleaning, a fire brigade and a police force) did not impress the *Criollos*. He was a patriot through and through, and would permit no interference in the Spanish control of their island. Very few Cubans were bidden to the

Left: Governor Miguel Tacón y Rosique.
Right: The Conde de Villanueva.

champagne parties that he gave on the roof of the new prison that he had caused to be built. Francisco Marty was one Creole who used to be invited, but his relationship with the governor was rather special, and anyway, he told good jokes.

Tacón's attitude towards the *Criollos* particularly aggravated the Cuban Conde de Villanueva, who held the position of administrator of the royal estates. During Tacón's administration the two men lived in a barely concealed state of animosity, which, as a result of the perceived expectations of high Havana society and extremely luckily for the city's development, found its expression in a contest of construction. Spanish/Creole one-upmanship gave Havana fountains, palaces, streets and railways. It was rumoured that the row had started when the Condesa de Villanueva had publicly snubbed the governor. In fact, the problem arose from the latter's hatred and distrust of the *Criollos* and from his overweening ego. When Tacón laid out the Campo de Marte military parade ground, he had four grandiose gates sited around its perimeter. These he named after Hernán Cortés, Pizarro and Christopher Columbus (Cristóbal Colón), reserving the main gates to be named after himself.

> With the great names, so respectable,
> Of Hernán Cortés and Colón
> Has mixed his own name, so detestable,
> Captain General Tacón[9]

fulminated an Habanero who, not surprisingly, wished to remain anonymous.

The empty hours of the Cuban gentleman, clever, wealthy and completely powerless, were filled with resentment of the Spanish yoke. Behind her smiling face *La Siempre Fidelísima Ciudad de La Habana* seethed with jealousies, enmities and impotent rage. 'The loyalty of Cuba is indeed a royal fiction,' wrote Maturin Ballou in 1854. 'As well might a highwayman praise the generosity of a rich traveller who surrenders his purse, watch and diamonds, at the muzzle of a pistol.'[10]

A major concern of the Creole sugar planters was that slavery should not be abolished. When it began to look as though Spain was likely to submit to British abolitionary pressure, further fuel was added to the smouldering coals of what was to become the movement for Cuban independence.

A Pompeian ceiling in the Palacio de Aldama.

The patio of the Palacio de Aldama.

Miguel de Aldama's sympathy with the movement was probably influenced by the slave trouble that he had himself experienced. On 9 October 1841 the slaves working on the construction of the Palacio de Aldama had rebelled, and the troops had had to be called out to suppress them. Then, during the 1860s, the slaves at one of the Aldama sugar mills went on strike, claiming that since they had arrived in Cuba after 1820 they were technically free and should, therefore, be paid. In 1868 a landowner called Carlos Manuel de Céspedes liberated the slaves on his plantation, the Demajagua. With his action the Ten Years' War was begun. Although it never spread from the eastern part of the island, it was to cause much suffering and expense to many of Havana's citizens, including Miguel de Aldama.

Forces of Spanish volunteers were raised to fight the rebels. They began to terrorize the people of Havana, and the authorities could not restrain them. The volunteers committed

174

A staircase in the Palacio de Aldama.

various atrocities, including gunning down some peaceful citizens as they were leaving the theatre. But the worst offence came when they accused a group of Havana medical students of desecrating the tomb of Gonzalo Castañón, the founder of the volunteer newspaper *La Voz de Cuba*. Apparently some scratches had been found on the piece of glass that covered the tomb. Forty-two students were arrested, but they were pronounced innocent and released. The volunteers were enraged, and tried the students by court martial. Eight students were shot at the Punta on 27 November 1871. The others received sentences of life imprisonment. Twenty years later, Castañón's son said that the marks on the tomb had been made by masons carrying out repairs.

176

José Martí.

Reticence on the part of the rebel commanders about their long-term intentions towards the slaves had gained them the financial support of several sugar planters, including Miguel de Aldama. The Spanish volunteers got to know of his activity in support of the Cuban rebels and resolved to attack him in his home. De Aldama was tipped off and managed to get out in time. When the volunteers burst in on 24 January 1869 they found the palace deserted, so they contented themselves with sacking it, shivering the great mirrors into fragments, ripping the paintings with their bayonets, firing their guns in all directions and reducing a fortune in fine furniture to matchwood.

The Ten Years' War ended unsatisfactorily in 1878 with the Peace of Zanjón. Miguel de Aldama's backing of the rebels had ruined him; when he died in 1888 he had returned to a similar state of poverty to that from which his father had emerged. His palace was later bought by an English syndicate for use as a cigar factory.

In 1853, one of Cuba's most important writers and thinkers, José Martí, was born in Havana at Calle Leonor Pérez number 14. When he was in his teens Martí was arrested for writing a letter that accused a friend of siding with the Spanish. In 1871 he was sent into exile in Spain. He began a writing career through which he continually called for Cuba's independence.

After living for some time in New York, Martí returned to Cuba in 1895 to fight for his beliefs, but on 19 May of that year he was killed at Dos Ríos in the province of Oriente. However, he had sounded a warning that was to echo in the minds of future generations of Cubans. 'It is my duty,' he wrote, 'to prevent through the independence of Cuba, the extension of the United States across the Antilles and their invasion of the other countries of our America with this added power.... I know the Monster, for I have lived in its lair.'[11]

However drunk he might become over a game of cards or however genial a conversation he might have with a smiling stranger in a restaurant, the first rule for every Habanero was to hold his tongue. The desire for independence was strong, but careless talk could cost him his freedom, at the very least. Anyone who made the slightest slip – an unguarded remark, a significant glance – might suddenly disappear as though he had never existed. Rumours of arrest and torture were whispered around the city. 'What fearful stories the dungeons of Moro could reveal had they tongue with which to speak!'[12] wrote Maturin Ballou in 1885.

But there were those in Havana who were serving a different sort of sentence. They were

Left: Habaneras.

Below: A silver gilt comb set with coral.

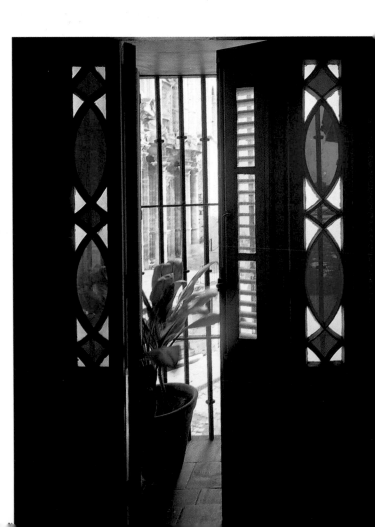

Above and right:
'Give me a kiss, Chinita!'. Iron bars were not always
an effective deterrent... but a house could feel
like a prison to those unwilling to risk censure.

not persecuted or tortured, but rather trapped in a strong cage of duty and tradition. Who knows, if they had been given their freedom whether they would have gathered up their skirts and grabbed a machete to fight for their country's longed-for independence? The situation could not possibly have arisen. The upper- and middle-class women of Havana were important symbols of wealth and social success, expensive treasures not to be lightly lost. Shut away like jewelled and painted icons, they were guarded and preserved from harm, respected, worshipped – and bored to distraction.

Habaneras never, ever walked through the streets. To do so would have been to commit a social solecism from which their reputations would never have recovered. They spent much of the day sitting in their rooms, idly chatting and toying with a little embroidery or playing the guitar. The windows that overlooked the pavement were heavily barred, supposedly to keep robbers out. Once a foreign sailor, on seeing the wistful faces peering out of what appeared to be a luxurious prison, tossed them a silver dollar and called to them to be of good heart. The remark was greeted with much hilarity, but it must have been tantalizing to see so much going on outside and not to be able to join in. When their mothers were not looking, the daughters of the house would sometimes step right into the box of bars round the window to receive flowers and even kisses from their beaux. If they were seen they were yanked back into the room with shrieks of maternal outrage.

The only reason for a lady to venture outside during the day would be to undertake a shopping expedition. The volanta, usually kept just inside the front door, would be ordered. This carriage was the ultimate in fashion accessories. Its floor would be carpeted with a Persian rug, on which stood a silver footrest. Crimson velvet screens, which could be let down to protect delicate complexions from darkening in the sun, were rolled up and fastened with blue and gold tasselled silk cords. The seat was black leather, studded with crimson velvet buttons. An enormous leather hood was decorated outside with silver filigree and inside with quilted black velvet and tiny red velvet bows. The huge wheels were crimson with a black trim, and the straps of the harness ran through coiled metal serpents on the long, smooth shafts.

The females of the house would descend the stairs in their full finery, climb into the carriage and be driven carefully to the shops. Here, they would not walk inside, for fear of being left alone with a member of the opposite sex. They waited regally in the volanta, while goods were carried out of the door for their inspection. Once the purchases had been made, they would be driven straight home again. The whole performance caused a great deal of fuss and bother, but it might mean as much as two hours outside the house, a release not to be sneered at. It is not surprising that ladies doted on their volantas. They were their only means of escape.

During the afternoon, if the ladies were very lucky, they might receive visitors. Strict formalities were observed when gentlemen came to pay a call. Two rows of chairs were lined up facing each other and running from each side of the window towards the centre of the room. The men sat in one row. The women sat opposite in the other. Woe betide anyone who crossed the dividing space between.

The situation was hardly conducive to lively conversation or shared intimacies. Formal courtesies were interspersed with long silences during which the ladies fluttered their fans. The gentlemen smoked cigars, held in silver or gold tongs so as not to soil their gloves. After one particular visit was lengthily concluded, a smitten youth went home and tore his hair over the composition of a long, adoring letter filled with all the things he had been unable to say: 'Your beautiful image had scarcely struck my retina by means of the convergent rays, when my heart was filled with hot blood, as if I had tasted the nectar of the Gods, or the heavenly ambrosia... &c. &c.'[13]

One can understand such florid prose when one sees paintings of young Habaneras. A picture hanging in the Palacio de Bellas Artes is an eighteenth-century portrait of a blue-eyed girl in a white dress trimmed with cream lace and blue silk bows. Ribbons are woven through her ringlets. She is wearing gold and diamond rings and diamond and sapphire earrings, and carrying a carved fan and a fluffy white lapdog. The expressions of both dog and girl exude flirtatious naughtiness, and the painting is inscribed 'Vicente Escovar painted me in 1797'.

Having little else to do, the women of Havana spent most of their time working on their appearance. Preparations for the excitements of the evening began early. Samuel Hazard implied, possibly unjustly, that the Habaneras were not over-keen to take baths. One lady remarked to him 'I say water is very bad for the body,'[14] and he related that wetting the corner of a towel with some *aguardiente* (rum) and rubbing it over her face and neck was the Habanera's favourite method of washing. Thus refreshed, she would call for her slave to dress her black hair in a heavy coil pinned up on top of her head with silver flowers. Next she would plaster her face with cascarilla, a mixture of finely powdered eggshells and egg white. Silk stockings would be rolled on and thin satin slippers selected. Finally her dress, a froth of flounced, ruffled, puffed and tucked silk or muslin, would be carefully lowered over her head. The accompanying jewellery was sometimes opals, garnets or pearls but usually diamonds. As the lady swept downstairs, her page would run to fetch her fan. To go out without it would have been unthinkable. In the coolness of the late afternoon, the volanta drove out of the door and turned towards the Paseo, carrying 'a great puff of blue or pink muslin or calico, extending over the sides to the shafts, topped off by a fan, with signs of a face behind it.'[15]

Driving smoothly up the wide avenue outside the walls, the Habanera would gracefully acknowledge her acquaintances. When a handsome man rode by on a high-stepping Andalusian stallion, she would make full use of her fan. 'She has a witching flirt with it that expresses scorn; a graceful wave of complaisance; an abrupt closing of it, that indicates

Setting out for an hour or two of decorous dalliance in the Paseo.

vexation or anger; a gradual and cautious opening of its folds, that signifies reluctant forgiveness.'[16]

At about seven o'clock, the Habanera would order her *calesero* (postilion) to drive her to the Plaza de Armas. Here there would be a tremendous crush of horses and carriages. The *caleseros* swore through gritted teeth and tried to force their way into the throng. Some of the volantas held two or three ladies and a little girl, dressed exactly like her mother, and already fluent in the language of the fan. She sat on a special seat in the front of the carriage, which actually came to be known as *la niña bonita*. The boys accompanied their fathers on foot or on horseback, dressed in perfectly tailored suits, wearing diamond rings and carrying a gold watch or a jewelled cane. The square was full of red and white camellias. Military musicians in bright uniforms marched up and down playing popular tunes. 'How ungrateful it would be,' mused a visitor 'to overthrow a governor whose band performs such delightful polkas, overtures and marches.'[17]

The ladies flirted outrageously, giggled frivolously and gossiped scandalously. The *Criollo* stalked about, exchanging stately salutations and lifting an eyebrow at the parvenu who, with one eye on his own wife and the other on everyone else's, sought introductions. He might prevail upon an acquaintance to present him to the leader of the Spanish set, the Conde de la Mortera, who had arrived in Cuba with his few possessions tied up in a handkerchief but had risen swiftly in the ranks of Havana's society thanks to excellent army contacts. Or he might bow to the queen of the rich Cuban clique, the Condesa de Fernandina – '*A los pies de usted, su Gracia*.' She had recently arrived from France, and her magnificent entertainments on the Champs-Elysées were much talked of. Of course, one knew that the Marquesa de Balboa and the Marquesa de O'Reilly were trying to compete with her, but their *tertulias* (semi-formal gatherings) would never rival her elegant levees.

Shortly before nine o'clock, the band lined up below the windows of the Palacio de los Capitanes Generales to play one last tune, just for the governor. Everybody began to debate the probem of how to spend the rest of the evening.

Havana at night must have looked like fairyland. The streets were full of the soft glow of the new glass lamps, and the waters of the harbour shone with phosphorescence. Light streamed from the doorway of the Café Dominica, a popular establishment which many people visited after the music in the Plaza de Armas had ended. Inside, little tables were set around a jasper fountain in a courtyard paved with marble. The chefs at the restaurant made over a hundred different preserves, which were exported all over the world, and produced liqueurs of every conceivable colour and flavour.

The ladies, who had no wish to ruin the paper-thin soles of their satin slippers by walking on them, sat outside in their volantas. The waiters rushed back and forth from kitchen to carriage with frosted glasses of *horchata* (almond milk sweetened with sugar), *agraz* (sharp, refreshing juice pressed from unripe grapes), *gara piña* (the pressed extract of pineapple rind fermented with sugar) and dishes of soursop ice cream with sweet biscuits.

From the Dominica, the Habaneras might drive to the theatre. At the Tacón they used to sit in a specially reserved area in the circle. Its little gate was guarded by several fierce old women. No husband, father, brother or fiancé was allowed into this sacred place. They brought refreshments for the ladies to the gate, from where they were passed on by the watchful *dueñas*.

The masked balls that were held in the city on Sunday nights were eagerly anticipated by Havana's cloistered beauties. 'They are passionately fond of dancing,' wrote Maturin Ballou, 'and tax the endurance of the gentlemen in their heroic worship of Terpsichore.'[18]

The gentlemen, who might have spent an exhausting afternoon in the arms of their mistresses, preferred to sit together and gamble. Even if the atmosphere did not remain amiable they were unfailingly discreet.

> When any man attending the ball, in his passion at a loss, or at an attempt to cheat, draws his knife and stabs another, he does it without a word of alarm, or any noise. The dealers of the cards do not stop, nor does a female scream. The only notice taken of the act, by the company present, is, that every one places his fore-finger across his lips, shuts his teeth and blows a long, stilling hiss; as much to say – '*never mention it*'.[19]

As many as 2,000 people might attend one ball in Havana; they were the most brilliant events. Early in the century everybody's favourite tune was the *contradanza*, a synthesis of Negro rhythms and French country dances brought from Haiti: 'a trance of sound, a rondo of constantly returning delicious melody, as nearly irresistible to the charmed sense as sound can be conceived to be.'[20] By the end of the 1880s the *contradanza* had evolved into the characteristically Cuban rhythm of the *danzón*.

The Habaneras used to attain bizarre heights of elegance for their evenings of dancing.

They adopted an ingenious method of adding sparkle to their costumes. When the sugar was harvested in the countryside, swarms of gigantic fireflies – *cocullos* – used to come out at night to feed on the cut cane, turning the fields into 'a sheet of tremulous phosphoric fire'.[21] The slaves on the plantations used to catch these insects in fine wicker cages, taking them to light their rooms, where lanterns and candles were not allowed. The free Negroes sold the insects in the markets, six for twenty-five cents. Each *cocullo* had a natural hook on its head. Ladies going to a ball would hang them in the flounces of their white ball-dresses and make belts out of them. Sometimes they would wear specially designed silver cages containing four or five *cocullos*. Attached to a bracelet or necklace, they looked just like pale emeralds.

The Habaneras, hung with diamonds and fireflies, with flowers in their hair and filigree fans in their hands, were a glorious sight. Their 'night-black eyes that alternately swim in melting lustre or sparkle in expressive glances'[22] apparently turned even the most hardened and practical of men into blithering romantic fools. When the ladies got home after the ball, the *cocullos* were carefully unhooked, put back in their cages and given a dish of cane juice.

By the nineteenth century the once-important religious observances in Havana had become little more than an opportunity for more socializing. Church on Sunday mornings was another excuse for the Habaneras to escape from the tedium of the house. They would go dressed in all their finery, attended by a slave who would precede his mistress into the church and lay a special carpet on the floor so that she might kneel down without dirtying her silks. The men sat high in the gallery. On Christmas night the view of the church from above, lit by a blaze of candle-light, had more to do with the sartorial than the sacred: 'Thousands of women, black, white, yellow, chocolate, coffee-coloured, most of them glittering with jewellery, half-submerged in waves of lace, knelt in a mingled crowd.'[23]

Religion was a tremendous comfort to the Habaneras, although not necessarily in the traditional sense. Many of them were visited by holy fathers, who went ostensibly to hear confession but frequently gave further cause for it. On one occasion the transaction between the priest and the pretty penitent did not go quite as planned. The reverend father had brought his dog with him. Unfortunately, the lady's husband had come home early. He was drunk, but not drunk enough to forget that he did not have a dog. A volley of barks greeted his knocking on her locked door, upon which he broke it down, rushed into the bedroom and bit his wife's nose half off.

If the women had to resort to subterfuge, the men openly visited the many brothels to be found in nineteenth-century Havana. Prostitutes, forbidden to solicit on the street, were also shut in behind the *rejas* like their more respectable sisters. However, they used to call out from their windows to likely clients, and in *Cuba with Pen and Pencil* Samuel Hazard tells of one unworldly foreign clergyman who on visiting the city was delighted to see that so many families in Havana were blessed with such great numbers of charming daughters. He greatly regretted that his poor Spanish prevented him from making their acquaintance. Most of these 'families' had houses in Calles Teniente Rey or Habana.

The behaviour of foreign females in Havana was considered shameless. Usually their offence amounted to nothing worse than being seen walking in the streets. But the names of girls like Rosamond Culbertson could not be mentioned in polite society.

Rosamond was dogged by bad luck before she came to the city and by bad judgement afterwards. She had run away from her American home to marry against her parents' wishes, but her husband died and she was left alone. Off she went to Cuba. If she was hoping to find a replacement husband she set about it in a peculiar way. Within a few days of arriving in Havana she had agreed to live under the protection of a priest, Father Manuel Canto of the San Francisco monastery. He established her in a house and gave her $500. Rosamond claimed that she would never have consented to the arrangement if she had known that Manuel was a priest, but even after having discovered the truth she did not seem particularly anxious to leave him.

Rosamond was either very confused, or very hypocritical, or a bad judge of character, or very brave, or completely immoral, or a mixture of all these qualities. Her *Narrative of the Captivity and Sufferings of an American Female under the Popish Priests* was written retrospectively from an exalted moral standpoint. But somehow the lady doth protest too much. What is quite clear is that Rosamond was as unsuited to living in sin as Manuel Canto was to his calling. There must have been many occasions on which the 'Popish Priest' wished that he had never met the 'American Female'!

At first, their relationship bowled along merrily. At Manuel's request, all their conversations were conducted in 'Champara', a combination of Spanish and African spoken among the Creoles. But when Rosamond caught the 'black vomit' (yellow fever) she suddenly realized that her way of life might be jeopardizing her passage to paradise. Manuel, the agreeable protector, suddenly found himself cast in the role of evil seducer. Rosamond lay on what everyone supposed would be her death bed. Manuel was most attentive, lighting candles everywhere to ensure a quick passage through purgatory, but his efforts were thwarted when an American friend of Rosamond's blew them all out, saying that they would drive the patient mad. Manuel's friends kindly came to see her, and they all entreated her to submit to a Catholic baptism in order to save her soul. Rosamond, temporarily reformed, branded them 'dissolute priests' and would not consider it.

When she recovered, the relationship continued, but Manuel began to stack up the odds against himself. During the daytime he wore a habit and acted the part of the model monk, but in the evening he would paint his face with rouge, put on a wig and wear extravagant evening dress – or worse: 'Manuel used to be very fond of appearing in the character of a lady.' He attended the public balls to dance and gamble, but it seemed that he only ever enjoyed a run of luck during the card games held at the monastery.

Rosamond fell ill again. Out came a long, tedious stream of accusations against Manuel, accompanied by more vows of reform. Then she returned to health and the arms of her transvestite monk. But at seven o'clock on the evening of 3 October 1828 the finger of judgement gave Rosamond another prod. Three robbers, a white, a black and a mulatto, broke into the house and attacked her. One of them went for her jewellery, and when he failed to open the catch on an earring she was wearing he tore it from Rosamond's lobe and stabbed her for good measure. Her friends told her later that her shrieks were heard in the Plaza de Armas. The commissaries came running. They plunged a sword into one of the intruders; the end of the weapon broke off, and he expired at Rosamond's feet. Later it was discovered that the men had been hired by one of Manuel's ex-girlfriends. She was a marquesa whom he had favoured with private 'confessions', and she had not taken kindly to being spurned.

When Rosamond recovered she moved to Calle Habana number 16, and began to threaten to leave her lover. Alternating between grief and rage at the prospect of losing her, Manuel declared that he would have her certified. However, she finally mustered enough resolution to run away from Havana, 'where they have every thing rich and splendid, horrid and wicked'.[24]

The clergy offered the ladies of Havana a number of services, but they were not very effective, and they sometimes led to disaster. A twenty-one-year-old woman called Marietta, who loved a dashing officer but had been forced to marry someone else, resolved to do away with her spouse. Off she trotted to her local priest, who obligingly sold her several curses and a few red candles to ensure their success. Marietta went through all the rigmarole required to bring about her husband's demise, but he remained disappointingly healthy. Not wishing to waste precious time, she proceeded to drug him with laudanum, stab him to death, cut him into manageable sections and cram him into a barrel.

Marietta's mistake had been to confide in her godmother, for that lady had promptly reported the matter to the authorities. Just as the widow sat down to light a relaxing cigar and contemplate the barrel with satisfaction, the commissaries arrived. They took the barrel away with them, and it was not long before Marietta found herself, dressed in white, being carried to the garrotte. She was surrounded by fifty priests carrying candles and crosses swathed in black crepe. It is to be hoped that the prayers they chanted did more to deliver her soul from damnation than their curses had done to dispatch her husband into oblivion.

Invitation, Enticement, Outrage, Reprimand, Forgiveness…
woe betide the gentleman who failed to understand
the language of the fan!

9

TRAVELLERS TO HAVANA

'The view of the harbour from the lighthouse is very good, quite worth the trouble of the visit. The fort itself I did not understand, but a young English officer, who was with me, pooh-poohed it as a thing of nothing. But then young English officers pooh-pooh everything.'

Anthony Trollope[1]

HAVANA HAS long possessed obvious attractions for the foreign visitor: a romantic and complex history, beautiful architecture, bright flowers, a baking sun, handsome people, a blue sea. However, she owes the special potency of her appeal to a quality that runs deeper than the stuff of which travel brochures are made. It is irresistible and intangible. Why should it be that such torrents of criticism and adoration have poured from the pens of so many visitors? How could they have lauded the city on one page and condemned it on the next? How is it possible that Havana's inhabitants can simultaneously be so thoroughly obstructive and so utterly charming? And why do so many foreigners still pray that they will never have the misfortune to go there again and yet declare in the same breath and with perfect truth that there is nowhere that they would rather be?

All rhetoric, for the answers lie in the impossibility of definition. However many times one visits there are always more discoveries, usually pleasant, seldom expected, to be made in Havana's streets, and the excitement of the search is hard to resist – as is the hunt through the Habaneros' baroque conversation for statements upon which one can rely, although after a week or two even the most diligent detective begins to spurn today's hard fact

The Hotel Inglaterra.

as tomorrow's fairytale. Habaneros adore mystery and continually do their damnedest to render everything even more intriguing, hilarious and exotic, and less intelligible, than it already is. There is no hope of beating them; they've had centuries of practice and conventional rules do not apply. Any strokes made against the tide are bound to be feeble – getting swept along with it is more fun, as many visitors have found.

Visitors began to flock to Havana in earnest during the nineteenth century. They recorded their trips in volume after volume of impressions, often confused and contradictory, but always vivid. Nobody could fail to be excited by their first view of the city. Sailing through the harbour mouth one passed so close to the towering Morro cliff one felt one might almost touch it. And suddenly the ship was in the port, surrounded on all sides by feverish activity, gleaming sails and fluttering pennants, all set against the backdrop of Havana's palms, columns and glowing colours.

Crowds of little boats would approach the incoming ship, rowed by thin Negroes in straw hats and blue and white checked shirts. Some were fruit sellers, their boats heaped with oranges and stalks of bananas. Others had been sent from the wharves to bring people ashore with their luggage. They nudged and jostled the side of the ship, vying for custom, but none of the passengers could leave until the vessel had been cleared by the health officer. This elegant individual arrived in his own good time in his own boat. He reclined languidly under an awning, wearing an immaculate white linen suit and a straw hat with a red band and smoking a long cigar.

Arriving at the San Francisco Wharf
by Federico Miahle.

The delay was tiresome to the excited visitors, but soon they were allowed to step down into the lighters and were rowed to the wharf. As soon as they set foot on dry land they were pounced upon from several directions at once by porters. Whichever was the most persistent swung the visitor's enormous trunk onto his head and stalked off through the teeming streets, with the flustered traveller scuttling along behind him, terrified of getting lost.

A hotel was to be trusted only if it was run by an American or a European; staying in a Cuban establishment was viewed by most visitors as an undesirable risk. The Inglaterra, facing the Parque de Isabela (now Parque Central), was a particular favourite. In 1884 the rooms cost the equivalent of 14s 6d (72½p) a day, but its facilities left a certain amount to be desired. The travellers' accounts reverberate with wails about the hard mattresses and the offhand service. The only way to get any attention was to open one's door and let out a loud shriek, 'repeated until the servant answers, or the caller gives up in despair'.[2]

Room service in Havana's hotels is still a little idiosyncratic, but it can at least be summoned by telephone. Even though one sometimes receives chocolate ice cream in response to a request for grilled fish, it is presented with such an engaging flourish of monogrammed plates and snowy napery that it seems churlish to press the point.

The Inglaterra has recently been restored and reopened. Its dining room and bar are cool havens of patterned tiles, potted palms and stained glass, and it is still a favourite with Havana's visitors. During the nineteenth century there was a cigar seller and a money changer in the lobby. The presence of the latter was no doubt greeted with relief. The currency was confusing in the extreme and travellers often fell prey to bamboozlement by quick-witted Cubans. Around 1850 the coins in circulation were dollars, quarter and half-dollars, both Spanish and Mexican, pesetas (then equivalent to about twenty cents) and silver reales (an eighth of a dollar). There were also two types of gold doubloon. The Mexican one was worth £3. 6s. 8d (£3.33) or $16, and the Spanish one was worth £3. 10s. 10d (£3.54) or $17. On top of all this there were many different notes of no value whatsoever in circulation, probably still wet from the presses whirring away in some cosy little courtyard in Old Havana. In his publication of 1850, Robert Baird sternly recommended all travellers contemplating a trip to Havana to buy a book showing detailed illustrations of every Cuban coin before their departure.

Once armed with a fistful of dollars, pesetas, reales and doubloons the visitor could sally forth to view the 'very unique but villainously odiferous city'.[3] They sometimes received the impression that every trader's sole aim in life in Havana was to part foreigners from their cash. Towards the end of the century the volantas, and their descendants the quitrins, had been joined by the more lumpish victorias. The rapacity of the drivers of these carriages was well known. The lamp-posts in the city were painted red in the central zone, blue in the intermediate area and green on the outskirts, to prevent the Jehus from charging for a greater distance than they had covered. The drivers made up for not being able to rook their clients by belting around the streets like charioteers, cutting corners and mounting pavements, a tradition faithfully maintained today by Havana taxi drivers. It was just as terrifying in the nineteenth century as it is in the twentieth: 'The wight who trusts himself to these conveyances may account himself fortunate if he does not come to grief more than thrice in two days,'[4] shuddered a victim.

Visitors to the city were fond of what the Habaneros considered the lunatic pursuit of sea bathing all year round. Special baths, with separate areas for women, men and Negroes were hewn out of the rocks along the coast. They were square, with seats below the water line and openings which, while letting the waves flow in and out, were 'small enough to prevent the ingress of any voracious monster of the deep'.[5] The worn remains of the baths can still be seen below the sea wall of the Malecón. The breakers rush over them ferociously, but the water is still as clear as air. It must have been delicious to while away hot afternoons under the striped awnings of the baths called 'The Elysian Fields', wriggling one's toes in the white sand and shells, and splashing in the gentle swirl of the waves.

Cuban cigars were famous the world over. An English gentleman, who sat 'under a canopy of Havannah', planning the itinerary of his trip in the hallowed hush of his club, would not omit from his plan a pilgrimage to the factory of La Honradez. Inside this famous establishment, which occupied an entire block between Calles Cuba and San Ignacio, were produced not only cigars but also 2,532,000 cigarettes each day. Upon arrival, the gentleman was requested to sign his name in a special book. During the time that it took him to see the factory, a personalized packet of cigarettes was produced and given to him as a souvenir of his visit.

While firms like Bock & Co. produced good, solid, traditional sounding brands of cigars like Pearl of the Pacific, Prince of Orange and Royal Engineers, some of the names that the other companies used were more than a trifle eccentric. José Candemil produced Drop of Water, Know Something and Plenty of Room. Estrada & Co. owned a brand coyly entitled For Me? Larrañaga & Co. sold a no-nonsense article called Ready & Rough. Eulogio González sweetly named his brand My Mother. Máximo Velez produced two madly contradictory varieties, Lord Palmerston and Slug, which Parets & Co. challenged with Hope Fulfilled and Dog. Thomas Salazar sold Happy Havana; Diego Trueba, Ultimatum; Vidal & Co., Perfection and Pretension. But Manuel de la Sala beat them all hollow with Bad, Extra Bad, Nothing is Worse and Don't Forget Me.

Nineteenth-century Havana was also a mecca for another type of pilgrim. Every year, droves of invalids from the north would stoically prepare themselves for the trials of a trip southwards, taking with them their medicines and pills, extra blankets, books full of advice on curing their maladies, more books listing the symptoms and cures for all the virulent diseases that they would be bound to catch on holiday, and countless changes of clothing to cope with every meteorological eventuality. Some spent their days sitting in their hotels, frail, pale and interesting, comparing agonies and inconveniences with fellow-sufferers. Others behaved with reckless daring: 'The first business was to put on woollen clothing, and

thick boots; which fairly prepared me to sally forth and see the city.'[6] Anybody who could walk around Havana's steaming streets encased in wool and leather must either have had the constitution of a rhinoceros or have spent the rest of their stay moaning faintly in a darkened room.

In the opinion of most of the sick list, their sojourn in the city was likely to prove fatal: 'The atmosphere appeared to me to be much better calculated to produce yellow fever than to restore diseased lungs, or otherwise produce benefit to *any* class of invalids.'[7] But Havana had been doctor's orders, and doctor, of course, knew best. So they stuck it out, martyrs in mosquito nets, in the daily expectation of meeting the bitter end.

Visitors to the city found the social customs of the Cubans quite extraordinary; a baffling combination of formality and friendliness. Almost every foreigner remarked upon how the people lived in the public eye, carrying on their everyday existence immediately behind the great windows open to the streets as though no one was looking. Cuban pedestrians were not usually looking; to them it was nothing remarkable. But the visitors would cast furtive and fascinated glances through the *rejas*, prey to the same insatiable curiosity that overtakes one when the neighbours forget to draw their curtains at night.

Every so often foreigners with letters of introduction were invited into Cuban houses for a visit or to attend a *tertulia*. These were gatherings held during the afternoon, at which the Habaneros listened to music recitals or poetry readings and smoked, man, woman and child, as though every cigar might be their last. 'It is really odd,' mused Maturin Ballou after experiencing an afternoon thick with the fragrant blue fumes of the Vuelta Abajo, 'that vessels don't scent Havana far out at sea before they heave in sight of its headlands.'[8] The Vuelta Abajo is a rural area in the province of Pinar del Río to the west of Havana where (the Cubans claim) the best tobacco in the world is grown.

As each guest came to the door, a rigid social ritual was performed. The new arrival would call out a series of salutations as he approached. He was then formally ushered into the midst of the gathering, where he paid elaborate respects to his hostess and her daughters. Once this process had been punctiliously observed, however, the protocol at an afternoon event was comparatively relaxed. 'It is less fatiguing than a tea party, being no more than a type of reception,' reported William Hurlbut. 'The main requirement for attendance at a reception is a pair of black pantaloons and a perpetual smile, for a Cuban tertulia, a perpetual smile, and a pair of white pantaloons will suffice.'[9]

Sometimes, however, all the flowery greetings and gracious smilings were contradicted by subsequent behaviour. The observer Francis Jameson greatly approved of the initial courtesies: 'All of this gives the impression of a lofty concept of salon manners,'[10] he wrote. But he added with dismay that he had seen one gentleman spitting with gay abandon all over the floor around his chair for the duration of his visit.

Some travellers to Havana seem to have gone there only to confirm their view that nowhere was as good as home. Their books are catalogues of complaints; moan, moan, moan, nothing was ever satisfactory. One young Englishman remarked from his high horse that Havana was 'the nastiest and most expensive hole in the world'.[11]

The tropical smells in the streets were a major source of distress. In 1871, a nitpicking Northerner described Havana's olfactory cocktail as being made up of 'smoke of tobacco, four parts; steam of garlic, three parts; aroma of Negro, two parts, miscellaneous garbage, one part'.[12] The noise of the city also wreaked havoc upon their fragile sensibilities. 'Even if the hapless stranger outlives the smells of Havannah he must in the long-run be killed by its sounds,' wrote another malcontent. 'For all the sugar in Cuba I declare that I would not fix my residence in a place where a man's nerves are put to such an excruciating daily and hourly trial.'[13]

It must be admitted that life in Havana was lived *fortissimo*. The combined effect of the babble from hundreds of cafés, casinos, clubs, bars and billiard rooms, the hooting ferries and mailboats, the church bells that rang periodically throughout the day, the grinding rumble of heavy wagons, the violins and guitars being scraped and twanged in all directions, the soldiers' stamping boots and blaring trumpets, the steamers, the buses, around 6,000 carriages clattering at top speed through the streets and all the endless chattering and shouting drove some visitors into a state of quivering despair.

Matters did not improve after dark. The evening cannon-shot heralded a city-wide crescendo as the Habaneros left their houses for a night of noisy fun. It was no good trying to escape from the racket by shutting oneself into one's hotel room; the sounds of joking and quarrelling in the courtyard, and the staff 'interminably washing and breaking dishes'[14] reverberated through the *rejas*. Even late at night, when the majority of the mob had shrilled their way home to bed, all the bells in the churches and castles still rang the quarter hours.

Any lingering prospect of sleep was finally dispelled by the nocturnal activities of street watchmen, old men in long overcoats with pistols stuck in their belts. Impervious to pleas and bribes, the *serenos* stumped up and down outside the foreigners' windows all night. Several times an hour they dealt the pavement a number of resounding whacks with their pikes and shouted the time and the state of the weather. They rounded the announcement off with a stentorian cry of 'All serene', an observation calculated to set the insomniac to shredding his sheets with his teeth.

These days Havana is quieter at night. There are those who lament the passing of the

HAVANA – *Portrait of a City*

cacophony which reached a climax during the first half of the twentieth century, but for dwellers in capitalist cities an unaccustomed dose of nocturnal peace can be a relief. Those suffering withdrawal symptoms can go and be deafened at a baseball game or spend an almost unbearably sensual evening dancing to Cuban music. But for the lovers, who sit in the moonlight on the sea wall along the Malecón, amorous murmuring and the crash and hiss of the breakers make a more intoxicating rhythm.

After their eventful nights, visitors blessed the lateness of the Cuban breakfast. Gentlemen in lightweight suits and ladies 'in fly-away muslins, and hair in the sweet neglect of the morning toilet'[15] gathered in the hotel dining room at about eleven o'clock to consume vast quantities of food: fruit, omelette, delicious baked fish with rice, fried plantain and a choice of meat dishes. The consensus of opinion among the travellers, as they washed it all down with claret and coffee, was that the food in Havana was delicious. But there were those who could not rest until they had found something to criticize: 'In my opinion, none of the fruits that they have here can be compared with those which we eat in England, … certainly many of the fruits considered good in Havana would only be given to the pigs in our country.'[16]

If this lady had spoken more Spanish she would have had a field day with one of the delicacies listed on the menus in Havana. It was called Ropa Vieja, and was a dish of beef stewed in a rich, savoury sauce. The visitors found it delicious until they realized that the name meant 'old clothes'.

This evocative concoction was usually eaten with rice for dinner. But it was sometimes difficult to get a mouthful of anything down your throat, because of the combined attentions of the various types of street vendors who were permitted to ply their trades in cafés and dining rooms. Shoeshine boys crawled about under the tables, polishing people's footwear. Trying to eat and maintain a conversation while invisible forces fiddled with one's feet was difficult enough, but periodically groups of musicians would surround the table and treat the diners to a rousing serenade. One would have to nod and smile with the Ropa Vieja sticking in one's throat and simultaneously fumble in one's pocket for coins to put in the tambourine that was being rattled purposefully under one's nose, while one's boots were buffeted and lottery-ticket sellers hissed mathematical blandishments in one's ear.

'From the first moment of setting foot on shore until the last before leaving,' expostulated John Mark in 1884, 'lottery tickets, lottery tickets, lottery tickets are fluttered before one's eyes at all places, and at all times – morning, noon and night.'[17] The vendors used to bear down on the unsuspecting foreigner, snapping the big scissors that they used to cut up the sheets of numbers, and lecture them at some length about the incredible potential of the particularly lucky combinations of numbers that they held.

Visitors to Havana also had to deal with hordes of persistent beggars. Most of them had a gimmick with which to draw attention to themselves: a parrot who sat on his master's shoulder and delicately took nuts from between his lips or a squirrel on a lead. One had a monkey, which ran up to passers-by and tugged at their sleeves with his little hairy paw. He would cast piteous looks up at them until they gave him some money, when he would scamper back to post the coins into his master's pocket. Maturin Ballou frequently passed a blind and dumb beggar on the corner of the flower market in Reina (Avenida Simón Bolívar):

> One morning a couple of roses and a sprig of lemon verbena were added to his small gratuity. The effect upon that sightless countenance was electrical, and the poor mendicant, having only panto-mime with which to express his delight, seemed half frantic. The money fell to the ground, but the flowers were pressed passionately to his breast.[18]

Another of Havana's beggars who wrung visitors' hearts, particularly those of the ladies, was a Creole with a devastatingly handsome face. His legs were withered and he sat on a street corner in a basket, but he wore an immaculate linen shirt with crisp ruffles, a silk cravat and gold studs. One look of appeal from his flashing black eyes would have women groping for their purses in a positive swoon of compassion.

If they had any money left after running the gauntlet of the beggars, the visitors would go to the shops to buy mementoes of their stay. There were walking sticks made out of sharks' vertebrae, piña cloth handkerchiefs, purses made from the skin of a snake called the maja, lacy shawls, cigars at $300 for a thousand, effigies of saints with squinting glass eyes and brocade robes, and the ubiquitous Cuban peasant hat which 'makes a good waste basket for papers'.[19]

Most of the ladies bought a fan. Skilled shopkeepers usually managed to talk them out of getting a cheap one on the grounds that it would prove to be 'dumb' and unable to convey any message to a gentleman. If one paid a little more one could purchase a more voluble version with a satisfying snap, guaranteed to seduce every man for miles. The most costly fans had carved ivory sticks inlaid with gold and mounted with tiny oval mirrors. Their silk folds were embroidered, hand-painted and scented.

During their inquisitive perambulations around the city, the visitors remarked over and over again on the singular appearance of the buildings and the streets: 'By this time, if not before, we began to realize that we were in a foreign city and land, with many scenes new to us, quaint, amusing and instructive'.[20] They were amazed at the warmth with which they

were welcomed by the Habaneros, and delighted by 'their universal habit of profuse compliment'.[21] They doted on the volantas: in *Due South, or Cuba Past and Present* Maturin Ballou wrote 'the motion is most agreeable, like being rocked in a cloud'. The public entertainments were praised to the skies: 'Nowhere can we conceive a musical performance listened to with more delightful relish than in the Plaza in Havana.'[22] They succumbed with sighs of pleasure to the soothing effects of the balmy atmosphere: 'mild and delicious... wonderfully transparent.'[23] They enthused about the theatre– 'I caught myself a number of times laughing heartily with the audience'[24] – about the satin-shod foot of the Habanera – 'a marvel of smallness and delicacy'[25] – about the ice cream – 'I thought it especially fine'[26] – about the

'Prophetic almanac for the year 1866: September. The gringos will invade Havana'.

waves against the sea wall – 'throwing up airy clouds of spray which floated off in rainbows'[27] – and about all the remarkable sights of 'wonderful, quaint and beautiful Havana'[28] at night, 'when the lights on the waterfront are reflected in quivering bars and bands of radiance from the water, and the lantern of the Morro glows and dims and glows again'.[29]

Just as much passion was devoted to expressions of violent dissatisfaction. The visitors winced at the sight of the chain gangs, bound at wrist and ankle, being driven down the streets in the blazing sun by overseers with whips. They started at the serpentine hissing with which the Habaneros attracted each other's attention: 'I have no doubt, if a fire were to break out at the next door, a Cuban would call "P-s-t".'[30] They railed against the fatalistic philosophy of *mañana*: 'You feel that to contend with it would be like dashing yourself against the barred doors of destiny.'[31] They disapproved drearily of the frivolity of Cuban women, 'overmuch addicted to cosmetics and meretricious ornament'.[32] They stopped their ears with pained expressions at the high pitched cries of the street vendors, which 'cause within you a disagreeable apprehension that some one is being murdered. But it is only one who sells eggs'.[33] They scattered with genteel squeals of distress when carts bore down on them, the drivers giving exasperated shouts of '¡Cuidado!' They sneered at the Habaneros' horror of the rain: 'When necessity compels them to appear, they walk with the peculiar circumspection of a cat, picking their way with a care and timidity that often seems highly ludicrous'.[34] One foreigner wanted to parade a volanta back home, but another said of the celebrated vehicle: 'it is a cross between a mule-litter and a wheel-barrow run backward, and possesses the great advantages of both.'[35]

The Cubans gave as good as they got. A cigarette label in the series 'Prophetic Almanac for the year 1886', issued by La Honradez, shows a comically overdressed Northern family coming ashore. Papa has woolly side whiskers, a tartan-trimmed cap and armfuls of unnecessary luggage. Frederick is supercilious, little Dorothea is fat and fractious, Mama has already located a whiff of drains. The title announces with weary resignation: 'September. The gringos will invade Havana.'

But even when, like the American George W. Carleton, they found a tarantula in their trunk on their last night, the Gringos kept coming back. They couldn't resist the Cubans' hospitality, creativity, kindness and charm, or their city's graces, mysteries and contradictions. A passing acquaintance with Havana becomes a lifelong attachment.

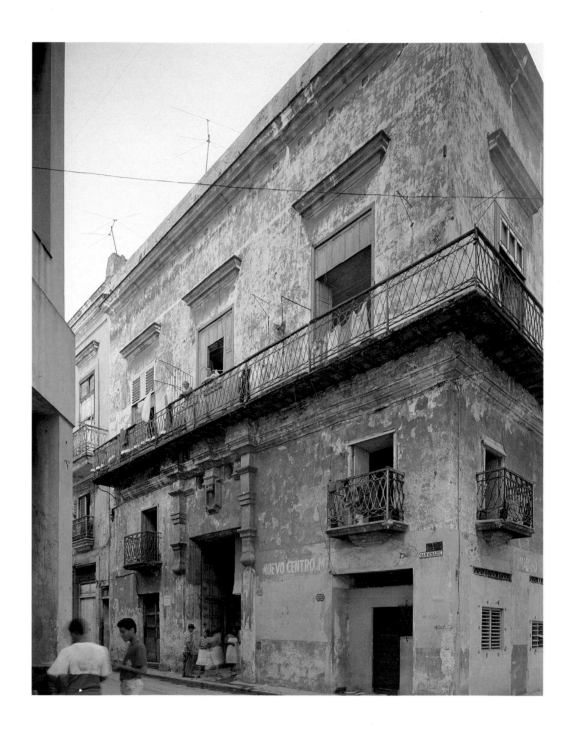

Above: An old house in La Habana Vieja before restoration: Calle San Ignacio number 202 on the corner of Calle Obra Pía.

Opposite: Calle Obra Pía. In 1982 Havana was declared a UNESCO World Heritage Site. Its hundreds of important buildings are being restored to extremely high standards.

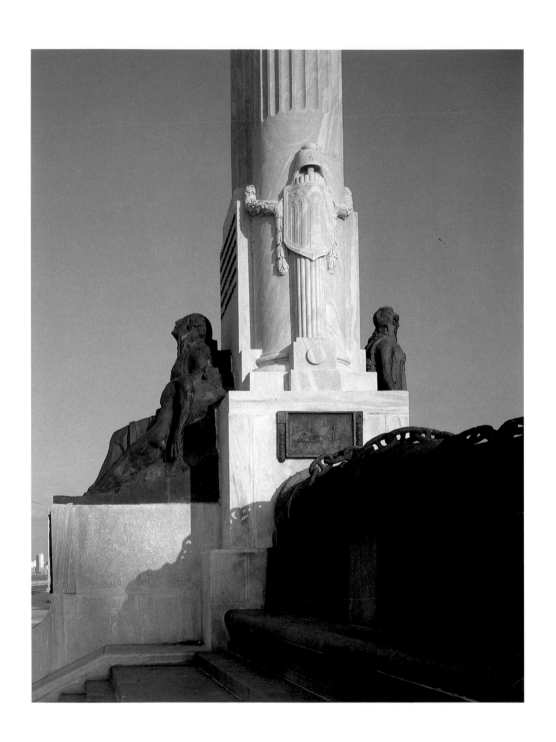

202   The monument to the victims of the *Maine*.

As the nineteenth century drew to a close Spain struggled to retain her hold on Cuba, and North America focused her gaze on the island's economic potential. William Randolph Hearst sent a journalist, Richard Harding Davis, and a cartoonist, Frederic Remington, to Havana as war correspondents. Remington sent a message to Hearst, saying that there wasn't going to be a war and he wanted to return. 'Please remain,' Hearst telegraphed back, 'You furnish the pictures and I'll furnish the war.'[1]

On 15 February 1898 the US battleship *Maine* exploded mysteriously in Havana harbour. Did the Americans blow up their own ship? The matter was never resolved, but it served as justification for the U.S. invasion of Cuba.

On 1 January 1899 the Spanish left the island. Two years later Cuba was proclaimed a republic, but in effect it became an American colony.

In the following decades Havana filled with milkshakes and mafiosi, hot dogs and whores. Yanqui Doodle had come to town and was having martini-drinking competitions in the Sevilla Bar. A replica of the Capitol building was built on the Prado, and La Habana Vieja crumbled in the sun.

204   Cuba's oldest postbox, in the Plaza de la Catedral.

NOTES

Chapter 1. Discoverers and Explorers

1. Letter of Columbus to various persons dated 15 February 1493 describing the results of his first voyage and written on the return journey. Quoted in: Cohen, J.M. (ed) *The Four Voyages of Christopher Columbus. Being his own log-book, letters and dispatches with connecting narrative drawn from the Life of the Admiral by his son Hernando Colón and other contemporary historians,* The Cresset Library, London, 1988, p. 119

2. De las Casas, Bartolomé, 'Digest of Columbus's log-book on his first voyage', entry for Sunday, 28 October 1492. Quoted in: Cohen, J.M. (ed), *op. cit.,* p. 76

3. Colón, Hernando, *The Life of the Admiral by his son,* Chapter 28. Quoted in: Cohen, J.M. (ed), *op. cit.,* p. 79

4. *A briefe Narration of the destruction of the Indies by the Spaniards: written by a Frier Bart. de las Casas a Spaniard, and Bishop of Chiapa in America.* In *Purchas his Pilgrimes,* The Fourth Part. Printed by William Stansby for Henrie Fetherstone and are to be sold at his shop in Pauls Church-yard at the signe of the Rose, [London], 1625, p. 1574

Chapter 2. Settlers – the Birth of a City

1. De la Parra, Hernando, 'Apuntaciones sobre la fundación y progresos de la Villa de la Habana, 1595' in *Protocolo de antigüedades, literatura, agricultura, industria, comercio, etc.,* Imprenta de M. Soler, Havana, 1845. Quoted in: Eguren, Gustavo, *La Fidelísima Habana,* Editorial Letras Cubanas, Havana, 1986, p. 109. *Hasta ahora yo no veo ... los prospectos de ricas minas con que se alucinó nuestra imaginación.* (I have not yet seen any signs of the rich mines with which our imaginations have been deluded.)

2. Relación del bachiller Alonso Parada a S.M., Julio 2 de 1527. Quoted in: Eguren, Gustavo, *op. cit.,* p. 20. *cada dia en mucha disminución* (diminishing every day)

3. Cabildo [town council decree], 1590. Pérez Beato, Manuel, 'Habana histórica y tradicional' in *Archivo del Folklore Cubano,* vol. 1, no. 3, Havana, 1925. Quoted in: Roig de Leuchsenring, Emilio, *Cuadernos de Historia Habanera, La Habana Antigua: La Plaza de Armas,* Havana, 1935, p. 11. *por el perjuicio a la salud y el mal olor de sus despojos* (because of the danger to health and the unpleasant smell of their remains)

4. Cabildo, Junio 19 de 1551 [town council decree, 19 June 1551]. Quoted in Eguren, Gustavo, *op. cit.,* p. 30. *Fue acordado que por quanto los negros que andan a jornal andan a traer ... uvas ... e naranjas ... sus amos son dañificados por que se azen holgaçanes por tanto mandaron pregonar publicamente que ningund negro ni negra de los que andan a jornal e se alquilan no pueda vender ... naranjas ni platanos ... ni uvas ni otra ninguna frutas ni otro ningund negro aunque no sea jornalero no lo pueda vender so pena quel que se hallare con ello e lo tragese para vender incurra en pena de trezientos açotes que le seran publicamente por las calles publicas desta villa e diez dias en la carçel con cepo e cadena.* (It is reported that Negro workers are collecting ... grapes ... and oranges ... their masters are thus inconvenienced by their slaves becoming idle ... it is thus publicly proclaimed that no Negro labourer may sell oranges nor bananas nor grapes nor any other fruits, nor may any other Negro who is not a labourer sell such items. If they are found in possession of such objects intending to sell them they will incur the penalty of three hundred lashes given publicly in the open streets of this town and ten days in prison, chained in the stocks.)

5. Cabildo, Abril 18 de 1551 [town council decree, 18 April 1551]. Quoted in: Eguren, Gustavo *op. cit.*, p. 28. *los taberneros que en esta villa rresiden tienen mucha deshorden en la manera de bender del bino* (the inns of this town are very disorderly)

6. Cabildo Junio 12 de 1567 [town council decree, 12 June 1567]. Quoted in: Eguren Gustavo, *op. cit.*, p. 51. *Por quanto ay mucho deshorden los Domingos e fiestas... en las tabernas e bodegones en dar de comer e vender vino antes de misa mayor se pregone publicamente que de aqui adelante ningund tabernero abra taberna ni venda vino ni ninguna persona hasta ser dicha e acabada la misa mayor.* (Since there is so much disorder on Sundays and festive days due to the inns selling wine and food before mass it is publicly ordered that no innkeeper may open his establishment or sell wine to anybody until after church.)

7. Ordenanzas del castillo de la Fuerza dictadas por Diego Fernández de Quiñones, Agosto 3 de 1582 [rules of the castle of the Fuerza dictated by Diego Fernández de Quiñones, 3 August 1582]. Quoted in: Eguren, Gustavo, *op. cit.* p. 79. *Que el soldado que en el juego o en otra qualquiera conversaçion blasfemare de nuestro señor o de nuestra señora o de sus santos este preso en el çepo los treynta dias que manda la ley e por la segunda ves otros treynta... e por la terçera vergüenza publica e a galeras por quatro años el Remo por blasfemo e mal christiano.* (Any soldier who while gambling or in general conversation speaks ill of our Lord or our Lady or the Saints will be placed in the stocks for thirty days as decreed by law, and the second time for another thirty days... and on the third disgraceful occasion he will be condemned to row in the galleys for four years, as a blasphemer and a bad Christian.)

8. Carta del licenciado Joanes de Ávila al Rey, Mayo 31 de 1545 [letter from governor to king, 31 May 1545]. Quoted in: Eguren, Gustavo, *op. cit.*, p. 24. *En esta villa de la Avana ay gran neseçidad de traerse el agua por los muchos navios que a ella ocurren e son tantos los que peresçen asy marineros como esclavos negros e yndios que si vuestra magestad no le faze merced de mandarle dar su çedula Real para que cada navio que aqui entrare pague de cada tonelada e negro que traxere... para el muelle para traer la dicha agua.* (In this town of Havana there is a pressing necessity to supply water to the large numbers of ships that arrive here, and so many sailors, black slaves and Indians die that we beg Your Majesty to issue a royal decree that every ship that enters this port pays a tariff for every ton of goods and every slave that it carries ... in order that we may construct a wharf from which to supply the said water)

9. Cabildo, Agosto 2 de 1568 [town council decree, 2 August 1568]. Quoted in: Eguren, Gustavo, *op. cit.*, p. 52. *Por quanto los bastimentos que se venden en esta villa de pan e frutas e otras legumbres se venden secretamente de lo qual rredunda daño e perjuiçio a la rrepublica e para el rremedio dello proveyron e mandaron que todas e qualesquier personas españoles como negros e yndios que hobieron de vender algund bastimento de pan de trigo e frutas hortaliças e otras legunbres lo vendan en las plaças publicas desta villa e no lo vendan en sus casas ni escondidamente so pena si fuere español de perder lo que ansi vendiere e mas tres ducados aplicados... si negro o negra o yndio o yndia el que ansi vendiere la dicha pena e si no tobiere de que pagalla que se le den çien açotes por las calles publicas por la premera vez e por la segunda la pena doblada e por la terçera de ser tres-doblada e un año de destierro desta villa.* (In as much as the provisions, bread, fruit and other vegetables for sale in this town are being sold secretly to the detriment of the republic, it is decreed that whatsoever person, Spanish, black or Indian, who intends to sell provisions such as bread and fruit and other vegetables must sell them in the public places of this town and not in their houses in secret, on pain, if they are Spanish, of confiscation of the goods they are selling and a fine of three ducados. ... If any black man or woman or Indian man or woman commits the said crime and has not the means to pay the fine they will receive one hundred lashes on the public streets for the first offence and this will be doubled for the second offence and trebled for the third and they will be banished from this town for one year.)

10. Fernández de Quiñones, Diego, Memorial del estado en que se queda la fortaleza de la Habana, Diciembre 1 de 1582 [description of the current condition of the fortress of Havana, 1 December 1582]. Quoted in: Eguren, Gustavo, *op. cit.*, p. 82. *Tambien se por boca del mismo governador que tiene diez e seys mill ducados puestos en España*

... *que tiene mucha cantidad de perlas oy en su poder vistas por mis ojos e su muger a dicho publicamente que tiene quatro mill ducados ganados en Reales en dos años que a estan en este ofiçio no es mala ganança si es permitida.* (I have heard it from the governor's own lips that he has 16,000 ducados in Spain... he has a great quantity of pearls that I have seen with my own eyes and his wife has declared publicly that he has earned 4,000 ducados in rents in two years, which would not be an unreasonable profit for this job if it were legal.)

11. Carta de Gabriel de Luján al Rey, Diciembre 23 de 1584 [letter to king, 23 December 1584]. Quoted in: Eguren, Gustavo, *op. cit.*, p. 87. *Por la obligaçion del offizio que tengo e descargo de mi conziençia hago saber a V.M. que el alcayde e su alfarez e sargento estan publicamente amanzebados con tres mugeres cassadas e con tanta publiçidad como si fueran sus mugeres.* (Under the obligations of the position that I hold and in order to disburden my conscience I am bound to inform Your Majesty that the mayor and his sergeant and second lieutenant are parading three married women in public as though they were their own wives.)

12. Real Cédula, Diciembre 10 de 1588 [Royal letters patent, 10 December 1588]. Quoted in: Eguren, Gustavo, *op. cit.*, p. 97. *Por cuanto habiendo entendido las discordias y diferencias que hubo entre Gabriel de Luján, mi gobernador de la Ysla de Cuba, y Diego Fernández de Quiñones, mi capitán y alcaide de la fortaleza de la Habana, y los inconvenientes y daños que de ello se siguieron y pudieran seguir, he acordado que en la dicha Ysla haya una sola cabeza a quien en las cosas de gobierno, guerra y justicia todos los que residieran en ella obedeszcan ... el Maestre de Campo Joan de Texeda, Caballero de la Orden de Santiago, os he promovido por mi gobernador de la dicha Ysla de Cuba.* (In as much as I have noted the discords and differences which exist between Gabriel de Luján, my governor of the island of Cuba, and Diego Fernández de Quiñones, my captain and mayor of the fortress of Havana, and the inconveniences and damages which have resulted from this and may yet result, I have decided that in the said island there will be only one person in whom the power in all matters of government, war and justice will reside... Field Marshal Juan de Tejeda, Knight of the Order of Santiago, whom I have declared to be my governor of the said island of Cuba.)

13. Real Cédula, Diciembre 20 de 1592 [Royal letters patent, 20 December 1592]. Quoted in: Eguren, Gustavo, *op. cit.*, p. 102. *Don Felipe, por la gracia de Dios Rey de Castilla, de León, de Aragón... Por cuanto teniendo consideración a lo que los vecinos y moradores de la villa de S. Cristobal de La Habana de la Ysla de Cuba me han servido en su defensa y resistencia contra los enemigos y que la dicha Villa es de las principales poblaciones de la dha. Ysla y donde residen mi Gobernador y Oficiales de mi Hacienda, deseo que se ennoblezca y aumente. Por la presente quiero y es mi voluntad que ahora y de aquí adelante para siempre jamás la dha. Villa sea y se intitule la Ciudad de San Cristobal de la Habana de la dha. Ysla de Cuba.* (Don Felipe, by the grace of God, King of Castile, of León, of Aragón... in consideration that the citizens and inhabitants of the town of San Cristóbal de La Habana in the island of Cuba have served me in its defence and resistance against enemies, and as the said town is among the principal settlements of the said island where my governor and officials of my estate reside I wish to ennoble and enlarge it. I therefore desire and decree that from now and henceforth for ever the said town will be entitled City of San Cristóbal de La Habana of the said island of Cuba.)

Chapter 3. Pirates and Privateers

1. Exquemeling, Alexander Olivier, *Bucaniers of America: Or, a true Account of the Most remarkable Assaults Committed of late years upon the Coasts of the West Indies*, William Crooke, London, 1684, pp. 79–80.
2. Carta del governador Gonzalo Pérez de Angulo al Rey, Diciembre 23 de 1555 [letter from governor to king, 23 December 1555]. Quoted in: Eguren, Gustavo, *op. cit.*, p. 40. *Repito mis suplicas porque se provea governador para esta ysla / Estoy cansado ansy de la cosecha desta tierra como destos ynfortunios.* (I repeat my supplications that a governor be provided for this island; I am weary of the harvest of this earth as well as these misfortunes.)
3. Weiss, Joaquín E., *La Arquitectura Colonial Cubana*, Editorial Letras Cubanas, Havana, 1979,

vol. I, p. 20. *pasaba sus días y noches jugando* (spent his days and nights in play)

4. Wright, Irene Aloha, *Cuba*, The Macmillan Company, New York, 1910, p. 29

5. El Rey da aviso del corsario Drake, Noviembre 24 de 1585 [letter from king to governor, 24 November 1585]. Quoted in: Eguren, Gustavo, *op. cit.*, p. 88. *Mi gobernador de la Ysla de Cuba: Francisco Draque, se cree para robar y hacer los daños que pudiera, había pasado a las Yndias con algunos navíos de armada, y conviniendo tanto al bien y seguridad de ellas que no estén desapercibidas y que sepan con tiempo su intento, He mandado despachar a todas partes y porque podría acudir os he querido dar aviso de ello y así, luego que recibais este despacho, poneis en orden la gente util para la guerra proveyéndola de las armas y demás cosas necesarias y fortaleciendo donde conviniere de manera que no se pudiere recibir daño ni hallar los enemigos en que facello... YO el Rey.* (My Governor of the Island of Cuba: Francisco Draque, it is believed in order to rob and cause whatever damage he can, has left for the Indies with several armed ships, and so that everything may be made secure and in order that you are not taken unawares and in order that you are aware of his intent in time, I have sent dispatches to all those that I wish to advise, thus after you have received this dispatch, put all those able to fight on alert and supply them with arms and whatever other items are considered necessary and fortify everything in a manner which will prevent any damage being done in order that the enemy may not do any harm.)

6. Acuerdos de la Junta de Guerra: acta del escribano público Martín Calvo de la Puerta, Junio 4 de 1586 [decree of council of war, 4 June 1586]. Quoted in: Eguren, Gustavo, *op. cit.*, p. 91. *toda la armada de françisco Draque* (the entire armed fleet of Francisco Draque)

7. Weiss, Joaquín E, *op. cit.*, 1979, vol.I, p. 39. *Que sin ellos es imposible hacerse estas fábricas si no es con doblada costa* (For without them it is impossible to carry out these works, unless it be at double the cost)

8. Exquemeling, Alexander Olivier, *op. cit.*, pp. 78–9.

9. Articles on board Captain John Phillips's ship *Revenge*. Quoted in: Johnson, Captain Charles, *A General History of the Pyrates, from their first Rise and Settlement in the Island of Providence, to the present Time*, printed for, and sold by T. Woodward, at the Half-Moon, over against St Dunstan's Church, Fleet-Street, [London], 1726, vol. I, p. 398

10. Gage, Thomas, *A New Survey of the West-India's or The English American his Travail by Sea and Land by the true and painful endeavour of Thomas Gage, Preacher of the word of God at Deal in the County of Kent*, printed by E. Cotes and sold by John Sweeting at the Angel in Popes-head-alley, [London], 1677, p. 201

11. Real Cédula [royal letters patent], 24 May 1634. Quoted in: Norton, Albert J., *Norton's Complete Hand-book of Havana and Cuba*, Rand, McNally & Co., Chicago, 1900, p. 54. *Llave del Nuevo Mundo y Antemural de las Indias Occidentales* (Key to the New World and Bulwark of the West Indies)

12. Roig de Leuchsenring, Emilio, *La Habana, Apuntes Históricos*, Havana, 1939, p. 79. *Usa de azur (campo azul); tres castillos (*El Morro, La Fuerza y La Punta*) de plata alineados en faja, cada uno almenado de cuatro merlones y donjonado (torreado) de una torre de homenaje almenada de tres merlones; el todo mazonado (las líneas que marcan la separación de los sillares o el material que los une), y aclarado (puertas y demás huecos) de sable (color negro). Debajo, una llave de oro (del nuevo mundo) en la misma disposición, con el anillo a diestra (a la derecha del escudo, o sea a la izquierda de quien lo mira) y el paletón hacia abajo. Al timbre, corona mural de oro, formada por un círculo murado con cuatro puertas (sólo visibles una al centro y media en cada extremidad) y cuatro aspilleras (dos visibles); y en un cuerpo superior, separado por un cordón, ocho torres almenadas (cuatro visibles) unidas por lienzos de muralla almenada.* (Azure in chief three towers *towered* fesswise Argent masoned Sable the greater towers having four merlons and the lesser having three and in base a Key ward to the sinister and downward Or. **NB** The English description of the arms of Havana was given by the College of Arms in London.)

Chapter 4. Building for Posterity

1. D'Arignon, Villiet, *Voyage du S... à la Havane, la Vera-Cruz et le Mexique, apud, (Nicholas Bourgeois), voyages intéressants dans différentes colonies*

françaises, espagnoles, anglaises, etc. Quoted in: Eguren, Gustavo, *op. cit.*, p. 149. *Es una ciudad muy extensa, de traza regular y de las mejor fortificadas de América ... Adórnanla muchos edificios públicos, iglesias y conventos ... en su puerto, uno de los más vastos y hermosos, sostiene el Rey de España una numerosa maestranza un arsenal y talleres destinadas á construir buques de guerra.* (It is a most extensive city, of regular plan; one of the best fortified in America.... It is adorned with many public buildings, churches and convents.... In its port, one of the most vast and beautiful, the King of Spain maintains a great dockyard, an arsenal and workshops for the construction of warships.)

2. Rosaín, Domingo, *Necrópolis de La Habana*, Imprenta El Trabajo, Havana, 1875, p. 128. Inscription on tomb of Diego de Compostela in the church of Santa Teresa: *Mortis horam diem novissium et aeternos annos in mentem habuit (Vivirá eternamente su memoria como el día de su muerte*/His memory will live eternally as at the day of his death)

3. De Arrate, Felix, Quoted in: Weiss, Joaquín E., *op. cit.*, 1979, vol. 1, p. 121. *la devoción de los negros libres* (the devotions of free Negroes)

4. Inscription in Iglesia del Espíritu Santo: *Quien procedió del fuego de la caridad yace bajo ceniza, para resucitar de la ceniza. Quien no supo de entierro, sabe ahora del polvo de la ceniza, ya que para que no pereciera el fuego, fue enterrado bajo la ceniza. Es Valdés, que soplando las cenizas del túmulo, renace nuevo fénex, padre de fecunda prole en el orbe. El Iltmo. y Rvdmp. DMD Gerónimo Valdés, que procede del solar de S. Basilio, desde que allí recibió sus primeras luces, vivió esparciéndolas. Viva por siempre, grande honor del pueblo cubano, quien llegó a su cima, como esplendor y ejemplo de padre. Salió del tiempo para conquistar la eternidad. Viva y disfrute de una eternidad feliz.* (He who proceeded from the fire of charity rests in the ashes, to rise from the ashes. He who knew no burial, now knows the dust of the ashes, for in order that the fire should not cease, he was buried in its ashes. It is Valdés who, blowing aside the ashes of the tomb, will be reborn a new phoenix, Father of the fruitful inheritors of the globe. The most illustrious and most reverend father Don Gerónimo Valdés, of the order of San Basilio, where he received the divine light, to the heights after the example of his Holy Father. He departed from our time to conquer eternity; eternal joy be unto him.)

5. Rosaín, Domingo, *op. cit.*, p. 119. *Ricos imitadle, indigentes bendecidle.* (Rich people emulate him; poor people bless him.)

6. Hurlbut, William H., *Gan-Eden: or, Pictures of Cuba*, John P. Jewett & Co., Boston, 1854, p. 171

7. Rosaín, Domingo, *op. cit.*, p. 323. *Te amo y no podría decir por qué.* (I love you and I don't know why.)

8. Carpentier, Alejo, *La Ciudad de las Columnas*, Editorial Letras Cubanas, Havana, 1982, p. 26. *emporio de columnas, selva de columnas, columnata infinita La Ciudad de las Columnas* (a warehouse for columns, a jungle of columns, columns to infinity)

Chapter 5. City Squares, the Nobility and their Palaces

1. Villaverde, Cirilo, *Cecilia Valdés, o la Loma del Ángel* (first published in 1882), Editorial Pueblo y Educación, Havana, 1990. Quote taken from vol. 2, fourth part, pp. 202–3. *Se dirigió una mañana temprano al mercado de la Plaza Vieja ... en el centro se alzaba una fuente de piedra, compuesta de un tazón y cuatro delfines que vertían con intermitencias chorros de agua turbia y gruesa que ... recogian afanosos los aguadores negros en barriles para venderla por la ciudad a razón de medio real de plata uno. De ese centro partían radios ... marcados por los puestos de los placeros, al ras del piso, en la apariencia sin orden ni clasificación ninguna, pues al lado de uno donde se vendía verduras u hortalizas, había otro de aves vivas, o de frutas, o de caza, o de raíces comestibles, o de pájaros de jaula ... o de pescados de río y mar, todavía en la cesta o nasa del bote pescador; o de carnes frescas servidas en tablas ordinarias montadas por sus cabezas en barriles o en tijeras movibles; y todo respirando humedad ... cáscaras de frutas y de maíz verde, plumas y barro; sin un cobertizo ni un toldo, ni una cara decente; campesinos y negros, mal vestidos unos, casi desnudos otros .. y encima el cielo azul .. en que aparecía uno que otro volador celaje, imitando, ya transparente cendal, ora las alas de ángeles invisibles.* (Early one morning she went to the market in the Plaza Vieja ... rising from the centre was a stone fountain composed of a wide bowl and four dolphins

dissemination of which he devoted his life, died in sanctity. He will live eternally in the homage of the Cuban people, he who attained the from which gushed intermittent streams of thick, muddy liquid which Negro water vendors eagerly collected in barrels to be sold throughout the city for half a silver real each. From this central point paths ... were defined by the stalls laid out on the ground by the traders without any apparent order or classification. One would be for vegetables, another for live poultry, or fruits, or game, or edible roots, or caged birds, or river and sea fish still in the fishermen's baskets, or freshly killed meat hung by its head in barrels or from hooks; everything breathed humidity ... fruit rinds and green maize husks, feathers and mud, without any covering or awning. There was not a decent face to be seen among the peasants and Negroes, some poorly dressed, others almost naked ... and above were the blue heavens ... in which the odd cloud appeared like the transparent, gauzy wing of an invisible angel.)

2. Weiss, Joaquín E., *op. cit.*, 1979, vol. 2, p. 84. *a imitación de Real Casa de Correos que se está construyendo magnífica en el lado norte* (in imitation of the Royal Post Office which has been magnificently constructed on the north side)

3. Leal Spengler, Eusebio, *La Habana, Ciudad Antigua*, Editorial Letras Cubanas, Havana, 1988, p. 31. Memorial tablet set in the wall of one of the galleries of the Palacio de los Capitanes Generales: *Hic finem fecit tormento bellico yn opinate percuss D. María Cepero año 1557. PR. NR. A.M.* (Accidentally injured by a weapon, Doña María de Cepero died here in 1557. Padre Nuestro, Ave María.)

4. Poem on Vermay's tombstone, now preserved in the Museo de la ciudad de La Habana in the Palacio de los Capitanes Generales.
Vermay reposa aquí. La lumbre pura
Del entusiasmo iluminó su mente;
Un alma tuvo cándida y ardiente,
De artista el corazón y la ternura.
Era pintor; sembrado en nuestro suelo
Dejó de su arte el jermen poderoso,
Y en todo pecho, blando y generoso
Amor profundo, turbación y duelo.
Here lies Vermay. The pure light

Of enthusiasm illuminated his mind;
His soul was honest and ardent,
He had the tender heart of the artist.
He was a painter who sowed in our land
The powerful seed of his art,
And in every gentle and generous heart
Left profound love, distress and sorrow.

5. Masse, E.M., *L'Isle de Cuba et La Havane*, Paris, 1825. Quoted in: *Arquitectura Cuba*, vol. 355–6, January/February 1983, pp. 32–3. *Yo solía ir a la Plaza Vieja. Allí me esperaban cosas horribles y un mal olor ... El tasajo, el tocino, toda esa carne de res o de puerco, medio seca, medio salada, medio corrompida, y tan desagradable de ver y tocar. Negras viejas, vendedoras de huevos o de carne, me asombraban por su excesiva gordura .. Vestían como lo hacían antaño casi todas las mujeres de esas colonias, con un refajo sencillo y una camisa de grandes pliegues muy escotada en la espalda ... M Bernardin de Saint Pierre ... dice que un coco, despojado de su fibra, ofrece con sus tres huecos un idéntico parecido ... con las partes anterior y posterior de una negra ... Si él hubiese visto los hombros tan gruesos y redondeados de las negras de la Plaza Vieja, ¿con qué los hubiera comparado?* (I used to go to the Plaza Vieja. There, ghastly things and a dreadful smell awaited me ... the *tasajo* [dried meat], the bacon, the beef and pork, half dried, half salted, half rotten and most disagreeable to see and touch. Old black women, sellers of eggs or meat, surprised me by their excessive fatness. ... They were dressed in the manner of colonial women of olden times, in a simple skirt and a shirt gathered in pleats at the shoulder. ... M. Bernardin de Saint Pierre ... says that a coconut, stripped of its fibre, has an identical appearance with its three holes, to the anterior and posterior parts of a Negress ... If he could have seen the round, fat shoulders of the Negresses in the Plaza Vieja, with what would he have compared them?)

6. Carpentier, Alejo, Quoted in: 'The Many Lives of Old Havana', *National Geographic Magazine*, vol. 176, no. 2, August 1989, p. 282

7. Gallenga, A., *The Pearl of the Antilles*, Chapman & Hall, London, 1873, p. 29

8. Real Cédula [royal letters patent], December 1793. Quoted in: Weiss, Joaquín E., *op. cit.*, 1979, vol. 2, p. 74. *Las bien labradas piedras de una iglesia*

de este fuste... están clamando desde sus muros por la distinción de catedral. (The beautifully carved stones of a church of this consequence ... are clamouring from their walls for the distinction of [the title of] cathedral.)

9. Norman, B. M., *Rambles by Land and Water or notes of travel in Cuba and Mexico*, Paine & Burgess, New York, 1845, p. 42

10. Hill, Robert T., *Cuba and Porto Rico with the other islands of the West Indies*, T. Fisher Unwin, London, 1898, p. 112. *O Restos é Ymagen del grande Colón!/Mil ciglos durad guardados en la Vrna/Y en remembransa de nuestra Nación.* (O remains and image of the great Columbus!/For a thousand ages stay preserved in this urn/In remembrance of our nation.)

Chapter 6. Havana Besieged and Captured

1. Letter of Major Smith, Governor of the Island of Providence, written after a visit to Havana in 1665. Quoted in: Ogilby, John, *America: Being the Latest and most accurate description of the New World; containing the Original of the Inhabitants, and the Remarkable Voyage thither. Collected from most Authentick Authors, Augmented with later Observations, and Adorn'd with Maps and Sculptures, by John Ogilby Esq; His Majesty's Cosmographer, Geographick Printer, and Master of the Revels in the kingdom of Ireland. London, printed by the Author, and are to be had at his House in White Fryers*, 1671, p. 336

2. Pezuela, Jacobo de la, *Historia de la Isla de Cuba*, New York, 1842. Quoted in: Pezuela, Jacobo de la, *Como vió Jacobo de la Pezuela la Toma de La Habana por los Ingleses* in *Colección del Bicentenario de 1762*, City Historian's Office, Havana, 1962, p. 27. *Qué es esto, señor Arana?/¡Qué ha de ser, señor!... Lo que yo vine a anunciar a V.S. quince días hace, atropellando todos los peligros, como buen vasallo del Rey y buen español.'* ('What is it, Señor Arana?'/'What else can it be, Sir, ... but that which I faced so many hardships to report to you fifteen days ago, as a dutiful vassal of the king and a good Spaniard.')

3. Wright, Robert, *Life of Major-General James Wolfe*, 1864, Chapter ix. Quoted in: Thomas, Hugh, *Cuba The Pursuit of Freedom*, Eyre & Spottiswoode Ltd, London, 1971.

4. Shirley, Governor William, New Providence,

Bahama Islands, to Admiral Sir George Pocock, 29 March 1762. Quoted in: Syrett, David (ed), *The Siege and Capture of Havana 1762*, Navy Records Society, London, 1970, p. 79

5. Pocock, Admiral, to John Gambier, President of the Governors' Council of the Bahama Islands, *Namur*, off River Chorera, 28 June 1762. Quoted in: Syrett, David (ed), *op. cit.*, p. 205.

6. Keppel, Sonia, *Three Brothers at Havana, 1762*, Michael Russell Ltd, England, 1981, pp. 35–6

7. Orders and signals relative to the landing of troops, 16 May 1762. Quoted in: Syrett, David (ed.), *op. cit.*, p. 158

8. Keppel, Augustus, to Admiral Sir George Pocock, off River Cojímar, 7 June 1762. Quoted in: Syrett, David (ed), *op. cit.*, p. 164

9. Knowles, Sir Charles. Quoted in: Keppel, Sonia, *op. cit.*, p. 40

10. Pocock, Admiral Sir George to George Keppel, third Earl of Albemarle, *Namur*, 12 June 1762. Quoted in: Syrett, David (ed), *op. cit.*, p. 187

11. Soundings off the Morro taken by the master of the *Culloden*, 11 June 1762. Quoted in: Syrett, David (ed), *op. cit.*, p. 185

12. Keppel, Augustus, to Admiral Sir George Pocock, Cojímar, 12 June 1762, 8.00 p.m. Quoted in: Syrett, David (ed), *op. cit.*, p. 187

13. Keppel, Augustus, to Admiral Sir George Pocock, 14 June 1762. Quoted in: Syrett, David (ed), *op. cit.*, p. 191

14. Keppel, Augustus, to Admiral Sir George Pocock, *Valiant*, Cojímar, 30 June 1762, 4.00 p.m. Quoted in: Syrett, David (ed), *op. cit.*, p. 210

15. Pocock, Admiral Sir George to George Keppel, third Earl of Albemarle, *Namur*, Chorrera, 2 July 1762. Quoted in: Syrett, David (ed), *op. cit.*, p. 221

16. Miller, James, *Memoirs of an Invalid*, Transcripts of the Amherst Papers, packet 54, file 43, Public Archives of Canada. Quoted in: Syrett, David (ed), *op. cit.*, p. xxix

17. Keppel, Augustus, to Admiral Sir George Pocock, *Valiant*, Cojímar, 6 July 1762. Quoted in: Syrett, David (ed), *op. cit.*, p. 225

18. George Keppel, third Earl of Albemarle to Admiral Sir George Pocock, *Valiant*, 5 July 1762. Quoted in: Syrett, David (ed), *op. cit.*, p. 224

19. Velasco, Luís de, to George Keppel, third Earl of Albemarle. Quoted in: Valdés, Antonio José, *¿Historia de Cuba o historia de La Habana?*,

Selección de textos por Hortensia Pichardo, Editorial de Ciencias Sociales, Havana, 1987, pp.145–6. *Los tratados de capitulaciones que V.E. me manda formar, con las ventajas que me produzca el honor, es uno de los muchos brillantes rasgos, que V.E. dispensa a su casi prisioneros, manifestando su excelente bizarría… no aspiro a inmortalizar mi nombre, sólo deseo derramar el postrer aliento en defensa de mi Soberano, no teniendo pequeña parte en este estímulo la honra de la nación y amor a la patria… sólo hallo un objeto por el cual tengo que agradecer a mi feliz estrella, esta es la alta honra en que me considero de poder darme a reconocer por uno de sus apasionados servidores.* (The treaty of capitulation that Your Excellency has invited me to draw up, with the advantages that this honour bestows upon me, is one of the estimable characteristics that Your Excellency displays to your possible prisoners, a sign of your great gallantry. … I do not aspire to immortalize my name, I only wish to pour out my last breath in the defence of my monarch, and the motivation for my actions is in no small part dictated by the honour due to my nation and by love of my homeland.… I only know of one reason for which I must thank my lucky star: the high honour in which I may be held in being remembered as one of your devoted servants.)

20. Letter from a Jesuit priest resident in Havana to Javier Bonilla, Seville, 12 December 1763. Quoted in: Eguren, Gustavo, *op. cit.*, p.167. *No es ponderable el dolor que recibió toda la ciudad con la perdida de el Morro; eran las cuatro de la tarde y aun mirando tremolar en el la bandera de San Jorge no se creia todavía.* (The city was inexpressibly grieved at the loss of the Morro. It was at four o'clock in the afternoon, and those who saw the flag of St George fluttering from the fort were unable to believe it.)
21. Keppel, Sonia, *op. cit.*, p.72
22. George Keppel, third Earl of Albemarle to Juan de Prado y Portocarrero, Headquarters, on the Island of Cuba, 9 August 1762. Quoted in: Syrett, David (ed), *op. cit.*, pp.283–4
23. Juan de Prado y Portocarrero to George Keppel, third Earl of Albemarle, Havana, 10 August 1762. Quoted in: Syrett, David (ed), *op. cit.*, p.284. The text is a British officer's translation of the Governor's letter; the original

letter has been lost.
24. Juan de Prado y Portocarrero to George Keppel, third Earl of Albemarle, 11 August 1762. Quoted in: Syrett, David (ed), *op. cit.*, p.286
25. George Keppel, third Earl of Albemarle and Admiral Sir George Pocock to Juan de Prado y Portocarrero, St Lazaro, 12 August 1762. Quoted in: Syrett, David (ed), *op. cit.*, p.288
26. Jústiz de Santa Ana, Marquesa de, *Dolorosa métrica espreción del sitio y entrega de La Havana, dirigida a N.C. Monarca el Señor Don Carlos Tercero* (lament sent to Carlos III). Quoted in: Lezama Lima, José, *Antología de la poesía cubana*, Consejo Nacional de Cultura, Havana, 1965, pp.156–7

… Tu Havana Capitulada?
tu en llanto? tu en exterminio?
tu yá en extraño dominio?
Que dolor! O Patria amada!
Por no verte enagenada
quantos se sacrificaron?
y quantos mas enbidiaron
tan feliz honrrosa suerte,
de que con sangre en la muerte,
tus exequias rubricaron?…
… Quantos demuestran señales
en cicatrices, y heridas,
por ti Havana recividas?
díganlo los Hospitales:
Guerra activa en tantos males
fué el objeto del deseo;
mas sugetos al bombeo
pausiva guerra tuvieron
y sin tomar armas fueron
del enemigo Trofeo.
Thou, Havana, capitulated?
Thou in tears? Thou exterminated?
Thou now under foreign domination?
O Sorrow, adored homeland!
How many sacrificed themselves
To prevent thy alienation?
And how many more envied
The happy and honourable fortune
Of marking thy passing
With a bloody death?
… How many can show the signs,
The scars and wounds,
Received for thee, Havana?
Only the hospitals can tell

If all the evils of active engagement
Were the objects of our desire,
But subjected as we were to
    bombardment
Our action was but passive
And without sufficient arms
We became a trophy of our enemies.

27. George Keppel, third Earl of Albemarle to Bishop Don Pedro Agustín Morell de Santa Cruz, 27 August 1762. Quoted in: Valdés, Antonio José, *op. cit.*, p. 81. *Ilmo. S.: La cantidad ofrecida al Oficial Comandante de la artillería de S.M.B., por las campanas de la ciudad, es tan despreciable, que me obliga a mostrar mi disgusto.* (Illustrious Sir, the payment offered to the officer in command of H.M. Artillery … is so negligible that I am obliged to demonstrate my disgust.)

28. George Keppel, third Earl of Albemarle to Bishop Don Pedro Agustín Morell de Santa Cruz, 19 October 1762. Quoted in: Eguren, Gustavo, *op. cit.*, p. 173. *Ilustrisimo Señor: Mucho siento el hallerme con la necesidad de recordar a V. Y. de lo que deve aver pensado diez ha. A saver. – Un presente de la Yglesia a el General de un exercito conquistadora: lo menos que V.Y. puede pensar a ofrecer por esta donativo es Cien mil pesos. Mis deseos es a vivir en mucho concordia con V.Y. y la Yglesia, lo cual he manifestado en cada ocasion hasta aora. Espero el no tener motivos para deviar de mis inclinaciones por descuida alguna de su parte. Dios guarde & V.L.M.& ALBEMARLE.* (Most illustrious Sir, I am sorry to be under the necessity of writing to your Lordship what ought to have been thought of some days ago, viz., a donation from the church to the Commander-in-Chief of the victorious army. The least that your Lordship can offer will be 100,000 pesos. I wish to live in peace with your Lordship and the church, as I have shown in all that has hitherto occurred, and I hope that your Lordship will not give me reason to alter my intention. I kiss your Lordship's hands.
Your humble servant, ALBEMARLE.

29. Bishop Don Pedro Agustín Morell de Santa Cruz to George Keppel, third Earl of Albemarle, 22 October 1762. Quoted in: Valdés, Antonio José, *op. cit.*, p. 84. *Excelentísimo Señor. Muy señor mío: entre cuatro y cinco de la tarde del día ayer, estuvo a visitarme de parte de V.E. una persona, cuyo nombre, apellido y nación ignoro. Solo sé que habla español aunque con resabios de extrangero, y que trae en las orejas unas argollitas de oro, a usanza de mugeres. Repare que en la conversación me trataba de usted. Advertile el modo distinguido, que debía usar conmigo. Respondióme que siempre me diría usted. Reflexioné entonces que esta terquedad podría fundarse en tener algun grado, que mereciese tratamiento de Señoría. Preguntéselo y contestó diciéndome no hallarse con otro, que el de tirar bombas en nombre de su Soberano. Continuó por fin su tema, despidiéndose con voces altas; y por que en todo lo referido ha faltado al respeto debido a mi dignidad, y es muy justo sea corregido conforme a su exceso, ocurro a la satisfacción de V.E. &c.* (Your Excellency. Yesterday afternoon, between four and five o'clock, I was visited on behalf of Your Excellency by a person, of whose christian name, surname and nationality I am ignorant. I only know that he speaks Spanish with a foreigner's bad pronunciation, and that he wears little gold rings in his ears as women do. I noted that in our conversation he addressed me as *usted*. I informed him of the respectful manner with which he should treat me. He replied that he would always address me in the *usted* form. I assume that this stubbornness indicates that his rank allows him courteous treatment. I asked him if this was so, and he replied that the only privilege he enjoyed was that of firing cannonballs on behalf of his King. He continued upon this theme at some length, and bade me farewell in a loud voice, and because his demeanour demonstrated a lack of respect for my dignity and it is appropriate that he be corrected, I depend on Your Excellency's fulfilling this duty.)

30. Pezuela, Jacobo de la, *op. cit.*, 1962, p. 82. *Que estaba su miserable cuerpo a la disposición de los herejes.* (That his miserable body was at the disposition of the heretics.)

31. Williams, Eric, *From Columbus to Castro: The History of the Caribbean 1492–1969*, Andre Deutsch, London, 1989, p. 94

Chapter 7. Slavery

1. Manzano, Juan Francisco, *Poems by a Slave in the island of Cuba, recently liberated; translated from the*

Spanish by R.R. Madden, M.D. with the history of the early life of the Negro poet, written by himself; to which are prefixed two pieces descriptive of Cuban slavery and the slave-traffic, by R.R.M. London, Thomas Ward & Co., 27 Paternoster Row; and may be had at the office of the British and Foreign Anti-slavery Society, 27 New Broad Street, 1840. 'Thirty Years', p. 101

2. Rojas, María Teresa de, *Indice y Extractos del Archivo de Protocolos de La Habana, 1578–1585*, Havana, 1947, pp. 46–7. *Venta a censo otorgada por Jerónimo de Rojas y Avellaneda, vecino de la Habana, a favor de Domingos Pereira, vecino también de desta villa... tres esclavos nombrados Antón, herrero, de naçión çepe de hedad de hasta treinta y cinco años, Francisco, marinero, de más de cuarenta años, de naçión carabalí, y Antonio ... de más de cinquenta años, por 1,200 ducados que es el precio en que se estimó el valor de la propiedades descritas... E los dichos esclavos de suso nonbrados vos los doy por ladrones e borrachos e coxos, e si alguna tacha o enfermedad paresçieren thener o aver thenido los dichos negros e cada vno dellos, con esa misma vos los doy e desde luego vos la señalo e nonbro para que por esta rrazón no podays rreclamar ni thengais rrecurso ni rremedio.* Febrero 1579. (Bill of sale given by Jerónimo de Rojas y Avellaneda, citizen of Havana, in favour of Domingos Pereira, also citizen of this town... three slaves, named Antón (metal worker) of the Cape nation, of the age of about thirty-five years, Francisco (sailor), of over forty years, of the Carabalí nation, and Antonio.. of over fifty years, for 1,200 ducados, being the price at which the value of the property is estimated.... If the said slaves of the above names prove to be thieves, or drunkards, or to be lame, or if they prove to have had or to have any infirmity, either all of them or any one of them, the terms of sale will still apply, and if all of them or any one of them prove to have any defects, the terms of sale will still apply because they have inspected, and there will thus be no future recourse or remedy to reclaim payment. February 1579.)

3. Beauvallet, Leon, *Rachel and the New World: a trip to the United States and Cuba 1856* (translated and edited by Colin Clair), Abelard-Schumann Ltd, London/New York/Toronto, 1967, p. 195

4. Gurney, Joseph John, *A Winter in the West Indies, described in familiar letters to Henry Clay, of Kentucky*, John Murray, London, 1840, p. 207

5. Philalethes, Demoticus, *Yankee Travels through the Island of Cuba*, D. Appleton & Co., New York, 1856, p. 11

6. Murray, The Hon. Amelia M., *Letters from the United States, Cuba and Canada*, John W. Parker & Son, London, 1856, p. 60 (volume 2)

7. Hazard, Samuel, *Cuba with Pen and Pencil*, Sampson Low, Marston, Low & Searle, London, 1873, p. 168

8. Barras y Prado, Antonio de las, *La Habana a mediados del Siglo XIX*, Imprenta de la Ciudad Lineal, Madrid, 1925, pp. 116–19.
*Es la mulata la fatal manzana
que al suelo arroja la fatal discordia.
Nueva Elena, la guerra le acompaña,
todo hombre es Paris, todo casa es Troya.*

*Brilla en su faz la circasiana gracia
la africana centella, su piel brota
y su normanda sangre se requema
en las venas calientes de la Etiopia.*

*Cuando al son de la lúgubre campana,
a la fosa su victima desciende,
la cruel mulata su cigarro enciende
y va an inmolar otro hombre a su placer.*

The mulatta is the fatal apple
That brought discord to the world.
New Helen, war accompanies her,
Every man a Paris, every house a Troy.

Circassian grace shines in her face,
African light glows from her skin
And her Norman blood smoulders
In the hot veins of Ethiopia.

When, to the lugubrious sound of the bell
Her victim is laid in his grave,
The cruel mulatta lights her cigar
And goes to immolate another man at her pleasure.

9. Manzano, Juan Francisco, *op. cit.*, p. 66
10. Manzano, Juan Francisco, *op. cit.*, p. 61
11. Manzano, Juan Francisco, *op. cit.*, p. 79
12. Manzano, Juan Francisco, *op. cit.*, p. 69
13. Manzano, Juan Francisco, *op. cit.*, pp. 66–8
14. Manzano, Juan Francisco, *op. cit.*, pp. 9–16

Chapter 8. Society in the Nineteenth Century

1. Heredia, José María. Quoted in: Hurlbut, William, *op. cit.*, p. 207
2. Hazard, Samuel, *op. cit.*, pp. 84–5
3. Hazard, Samuel, *op. cit.*, p. 57
4. Hazard, Samuel, *op. cit.*, p. 195
5. Ballou, Maturin M., *History of Cuba; or, Notes of a Traveller in the Tropics. Being a Political, Historical and Statistical Account of the island, from its first discovery to the present time*, Phillips, Sampson & Co., New York, 1854, pp. 101–2
6. Jay, W.M.L. (J.L.M. Woodruff), *My Winter in Cuba*, E.P. Dutton & Co., New York, 1871, p. 73
7. Rosaín, Domingo, *op. cit.*, p. 219. *que llenos de columnas, adornos, dorados y molduras ... dando oscuridad y estrechez al lugar en que oraban los fieles* (which, full of columns, decorations, gilding and mouldings ... darken and dominate the places in which the faithful pray)
8. Hazard, Samuel, *op. cit.*, p. 143
9. Chateloin, Felicia, *La Habana de Tacón*, Editorial Letras Cubanas, Havana, 1989, p. 88. *Con el nombre respetable / de Hernán Cortés, y Colón / ha confundido Tacón / el suyo, tan detestable.* (With the great names, so respectable, / Of Hernán Cortés and Colón / Has mixed his own name, so detestable, / Captain General Tacón.)
10. Ballou, Maturin M. *op. cit.*, 1854, pp. 99–100.
11. Martí, José (the last letter he wrote, it was addressed to his friend Manuel Mercado but was unfinished). Quoted in: Thomas, Hugh, *op. cit.*, p. 310
12. Ballou, Maturin M., *Due South, or Cuba Past and Present*, Houghton, Mifflin & Co., Boston and New York, 1885, p. 167
13. Philalethes, Demoticus, *op. cit.*, p. 18.
14. Hazard, Samuel, *op. cit.*, p. 51
15. Dana Jr, Richard Henry, *To Cuba and Back. A Vacation Voyage*, Ticknor & Fields, Boston, 1859, p. 34
16. Ballou, Maturin M., *op. cit.*, 1854, p. 120
17. Ballou, Maturin M., *op. cit.*, 1854, p. 85
18. Ballou, Maturin M., *op. cit.*, 1854, p. 78
19. Culbertson, Rosamond, *Rosamond Culbertson: or, a Narrative of the Captivity and Sufferings of an American Female under the Popish Priests, in the Island of Cuba; with a full disclosure of their Manners and Customs. Written by Herself*, James S. Hodson, London, 1837, p. 178
20. Dana Jr, Richard Henry, *op. cit.*, p. 178
21. Wurdermann, Dr J.G.F. ('A Physician'), *Notes on Cuba*, James Munroe & Co., Boston, 1844, p. 287
22. Ballou, Maturin M., *op. cit.*, 1854, p. 78
23. Beauvallet, Leon, *op. cit.*, p. 186
24. Culbertson, Rosamond, *op. cit.*, p. 26

Chapter 9 Travellers to Havana

1. Trollope, Anthony, *The West Indies and the Spanish Main* (first published in 1859), Alan Sutton, Gloucester, 1985, p. 116
2. Dana Jr, Richard Henry, *op. cit.*, p. 61
3. Baird, Robert, *Impressions and Experiences of the West Indies and North America in 1849*, William Blackwood & Sons, Edinburgh and London, 1850, p. 175
4. Gallenga, A., *op. cit.*, p. 26
5. Hazard, Samuel, *op. cit.*, p. 53
6. Invalid, An, *A Winter in the West Indies and Florida with a particular description of St Croix, Trinidad de Cuba, Havana, Key West and St Augustine as places of resort for Northern invalids*, Wiley & Putnam, New York, 1839, p. 109
7. Invalid, An, *op. cit.*, p. 111
8. Ballou, Maturin M., *op. cit.*, 1854, p. 171
9. Hurlbut, William, *op. cit.*, p. 51
10. Jameson, Francis Robert, *Cartas Habaneras – Revista de la Biblioteca Nacional José Martí*, July / September 1966. Quoted in: Eguren, Gustavo, *op. cit.*, p. 217. *Todo esto da la impresión de un alto concepto de los modales de salón.* (All of this gives the impression of a lofty concept of salon manners.)
11. Gallenga, A., *op. cit.*, p. 25
12. Jay, W.M.L., *op. cit.*, p. 73
13. Gallenga, A., *op. cit.*, pp. 34–5
14. Dana Jr, Richard Henry *op. cit.*, p. 75
15. Dana Jr, Richard Henry, *op. cit.*, p. 43
16. Houston, Mrs, *Texas and The Gulf of Mexico*, London, 1844. Quoted in: Eguren, Gustavo, *op. cit.*, p. 276. *En mi opinión, ninguna de las frutas de aquí se puede comparar con las que comemos en Inglaterra, ... ciertamente, muchas de las frutas consideradas como buenas en La Habana se las darían unicamente a los puercos en nuestro país.* (In my opinion, none of the fruits that they have here can be compared with those which we eat in England, ... certainly many of the fruits considered good in Havana would only be given

to the pigs in our country.)

17. Mark, John, *My Trip to America and Havana in October and November 1884*, J.E. Cornish, Manchester, 1884, p. 71
18. Ballou, Maturin M., *op. cit.*, 1885, pp. 233–4
19. Foster & Reynolds, *Standard Guide to Havana*, Diamond News Co., New York, 1905, p. 36
20. Norton, Albert J., *op. cit.*, p. 34
21. Ballou, Maturin M., *op. cit.*, 1854, p. 117
22. Ballou, Maturin M., *op. cit.*, 1854, p. 86
23. Foster & Reynolds, *op. cit.*, p. 96
24. Norton, Albert J. *op. cit.*, p. 63
25. Ballou, Maturin M., *op. cit.*, 1854, p. 77
26. Norton, Albert J., *op. cit.*, p. 165
27. Norton, Albert J., *op. cit.*, p. 100
28. Norton, Albert J., *op. cit.*, p. 178

29. Foster & Reynolds, *op. cit.*, p. 52
30. Dana Jr, Richard Henry, *op. cit.*, p. 208
31. Hurlbut, William, *op. cit.*, p. 175
32. Fiske, Amos Kidder, *A history of the islands of the West Indian archipelago, together with an account of their physical characteristics, natural resources and present condition*, G.P. Putnam's Sons, New York and London, 1899, p. 20
33. Steele, James W., *Cuban Sketches*, G.P. Putnam's Sons, New York, 1881, p. 20
34. Norman B. M., *op. cit.* p. 34
35. Steele, James W., *op. cit.*, pp. 17–18

Postscript
1. Thomas, Hugh, *op. cit.*, p. 340

BIBLIOGRAPHY

Barras y Prado, Antonio de las, *La Habana a mediados del Siglo XIX*, Imprenta de la Ciudad Lineal, Madrid, 1925

Barreras Gutiérrez, Diana, *Voluptuosidad y Equilibrio en dos centros históricos*, Unpublished research, 1990

Beauvallet, Leon, *Rachel and the New World: a trip to the United States and Cuba*, first published in 1856 by Dix, Edwards & Co., New York; new edition (translated and edited by Colin Clair), Abelard-Schumann Ltd, London/New York/Toronto, 1967

Carpentier, Alejo, *La Ciudad de las Columnas*, Editorial Letras Cubanas, Havana, 1982

Chateloin, Felicia, *La Habana de Tacón*, Editorial Letras Cubanas, Havana, 1989

Cohen, J.M. (ed), *The Four Voyages of Christopher Columbus. Being his own log-book, letters and dispatches with connecting narrative drawn from the Life of the Admiral by his son Hernando Colón and other contemporary historians*, The Cresset Library, London, 1988

Eguren, Gustavo, *La Fidelísima Habana*, Editorial Letras Cubanas, Havana, 1986

Ellis, Keith, *Cuba's Nicolás Guillén, Poetry and Ideology*, University of Toronto Press, 1985

Foster & Reynolds, *Standard Guide to Havana*, Diamond News Co., New York, 1905

Gómez Alvarez, Máximo and Rodríguez Villamil, Marcos, *Guanabacoa ante la invasión de 1762: Mitos y Realidades*, Unpublished research, 1990

Haring, C.H., *The Buccaneers in the West Indies in the XVII Century*, Methuen & Co. Ltd, London, 1910

Hart, Francis Russell, *The Siege of Havana 1762*, George Allen & Unwin Ltd, London, 1931

Keppel, Sonia, *Three Brothers at Havana, 1762*, Michael Russell Ltd, England, 1981

Leal Spengler, Eusebio, *La Habana, Ciudad Antigua*, Editorial Letras Cubanas, Havana, 1988

Lewis, Barry and Marshall, Peter, *Into Cuba*, Zena Publications Ltd, London, 1985

Lezama Lima, José, *Antología de la poesía cubana*, Editorial de Consejo Nacional de Cuba, Havana, 1965

Méndez-Plasencia, Miriam and Suárez, Margarita, *Museo de Arte Colonial*, Editorial Letras Cubanas, Havana, 1985

Moreno Fraginals, Manuel and Fernández Reboiro, Antonio, *La Habana*, Colegio de Arquitectos de Cuba, Havana, 1963

Norton, Albert J., *Norton's Complete Hand-book of Havana and Cuba*, Rand, McNally & Co., Chicago, 1900

Núñez Jiménez, Antonio, *Cuba en las marquillas cigarreras del siglo XIX*, Ediciones turísticas de Cuba, Havana, 1985

Pereira, Manuel, 'Enchanted Seashell', *UNESCO Courier*, July 1984

Pérez Beato, Manuel, *Habana antigua, apuntes históricos*, Imprenta Seoane & Fernández y ca, Havana, 1936

Pezuela, Jacobo de la, *Como vió Jacoba de la Pezuela la Toma de La Habana por los Ingleses* in *Colección del Bicentenario de 1762*, City Historian's Office, Havana, 1962

Pichardo, Hortensia, *Facetas de Nuestra Historia*, Editorial Oriente, Santiago de Cuba, 1989

Robinson, Albert G., *Cuba Old and New*, Longmans Green and Co. New York, 1916

Roig de Leuchsenring, Emilio, *Cuadernos de Historia Habanera, La Habana Antigua: La Plaza de Armas*, Havana, 1935

Roig de Leuchsenring, Emilio, *La Habana, Apuntes Históricos*, Havana, 1939

Rojas, María Teresa de, *Indice y Extractos del Archivo de Protocolos de La Habana, 1578–1585*, Havana, 1947

Syrett, David (ed), *The Siege and Capture of Havana 1762*, Navy Records Society, London, 1970

Terry, T. Philip, *Terry's Guide to Cuba: including the Isle of Pines with a chapter on the ocean routes to the island. A Handbook for Travellers, with 2 specially drawn maps and 7 plans*, Houghton, Mifflin Co., Boston and New York, 1926

Thomas, Hugh, *Cuba The Pursuit of Freedom*, Eyre & Spottiswoode Ltd, London, 1971

Trollope, Anthony, *The West Indies and the Spanish Main* (first published in 1859), Alan Sutton, Gloucester, 1985

Valdés, Antonio José, *¿Historia de Cuba o historia de La Habana?*, Selección de textos por Hortensia Pichardo, Editorial de Ciencias Sociales, Havana, 1987

Villaverde, Cirilo, *Cecilia Valdés, o la Loma del Ángel* (first published in 1882), Editorial Pueblo y Educación, Havana, 1990 (two volumes)

Weiss y Sánchez, Joaquín E., *La Arquitectura Cubana del Siglo XIX*, Publicaciones de la Junta Nacional de Arqueología y Etnología, Havana, 1960

Weiss, Joaquín E., *La Arquitectura Colonial Cubana*, Editorial Letras Cubanas, Havana, 1979 (two volumes)

Williams, Eric, *From Columbus to Castro: The History of the Caribbean 1492–1969*, Andre Deutsch, London, 1989

Wright, Irene Aloha, *Cuba*, The Macmillan Company, New York, 1910

Wright, Irene Aloha, *The Early History of Cuba: 1492–1586*, The Macmillan Company, New York, 1916

Wright, Irene Aloha, *Historia documentada de San Cristóbal de La Habana en la Primera Mitad del Siglo XVII*, Academia de la Historia de Cuba, Havana, 1930

Journals
Arquitectura Cuba
Cuba Internacional
UNESCO Courier
National Geographic

The following titles were published before 1900 and may be difficult to obtain:

Andueza, J.M., *Isla de Cuba pintoresca, histórica, política, literaria, mercantil é industrial. Recuerdos, apuntes, impresiones de dos épocas* (edited by Boix), Impresor y Librero, Calle de Carretas no. 8, Madrid, 1841

Baird, Robert, *Impressions and Experiences of the West Indies and North America in 1849*, William Blackwood & Sons, Edinburgh and London, 1850

Ballou, Maturin M., *History of Cuba: or, Notes of a Traveller in the Tropics. Being a Political, Historical and Statistical Account of the island, from its first discovery to the present time*, Phillips, Sampson & Co., New York, 1854

Ballou, Maturin M., *Due South, or Cuba Past and Present*, Houghton, Mifflin & Co., Boston and New York, 1885

Barclay, Alexander, *A Practical View of the Present State of Slavery in the West Indies*, Smith, Elder & Co., London, 1826

Carleton, George W., *Our Artist in Cuba. Leaves from the sketch-book of a traveller during the winter of 1864–5* Carleton, New York, 1865

Casas, Bartolomé de las, *A briefe Narration of the destruction of the Indies by the Spaniards: written by a Frier Bart. de las Casas a Spaniard, and Bishop of Chiapa in America* in *Purchas his Pilgrimes*, The Fourth Part. Printed by William Stansby for Henrie Featherstone and are to be sold at his shop in Pauls Church-yard at the signe of the Rose, [London], 1625

Clark, William, J., *Commercial Cuba: A Book for Business Men*, Chapman and Hall Limited, London, 1899

Culbertson, Rosamond, *Rosamond Culbertson: or, a Narrative of the Captivity and Sufferings of an American Female under the Popish Priests, in the Island of Cuba; with a full disclosure of their Manners and Customs. Written by Herself*, James S. Hodson, London, 1837

Dana Jr, Richard Henry, *To Cuba and Back. A Vacation Voyage*, Ticknor & Fields, Boston, 1859

Exquemeling, Alexander Olivier, *Bucaniers of America: Or, a true Account of the Most remarkable Assaults Committed of late years upon the Coasts of the West Indies*, William Crooke, London, 1684

Fiske, Amos Kidder, *A history of the islands of the West Indian archipelago, together with an account of their physical characteristics, natural resources and present condition*, G.P. Putnam's Sons, New York and London, 1899

Gage, Thomas, *A New Survey of the West-India's or The English American his Travail by Sea and Land by the true and painful endeavour of Thomas Gage, Preacher of the word of God at Deal in the County of Kent*, printed by E. Cotes and sold by John Sweeting at the Angel in Popes-head-alley, [London], 1677

Gallenga, A., *The Pearl of the Antilles*, Chapman & Hall, London, 1873

Gurney, Joseph John, *A Winter in the West Indies, described in familiar letters to Henry Clay, of Kentucky*, John Murray, London, 1840

Hawkes, J., *A Steam Trip to the Tropics*, Charles J. Skeet, London, 1846

Hazard, Samuel, *Cuba with Pen and Pencil*, Sampson Low, Marston, Low & Searle, London, 1873

Hill, Robert T., *Cuba and Porto Rico with the other islands of the West Indies*, T. Fisher Unwin, London, 1898

Humboldt, Alexander, *The Island of Cuba* (translated by J.S. Thrasher), Derby & Jackson, New York, 1856

Hurlbut, William H., *Gan-Eden: or, Pictures of Cuba*, John P. Jewett & Co., Boston, 1854

Invalid, An, *A Winter in the West Indies and Florida with a particular description of St Croix, Trinidad de Cuba, Havana, Key West and St Augustine as places of resort for Northern invalids*, Wiley & Putnam, New York, 1839

Jay, W.M.L. (J.L.M. Woodruff), *My Winter in Cuba*, E.P. Dutton & Co., New York, 1871

Johnson, Captain Charles, *A General History of the Pyrates, from Their first Rise and Settlement in the Island of Providence, to the present Time*, printed for, and sold by T. Woodward, at the Half-Moon, over against

St Dunstan's Church, Fleet-Street, [London], 1726

Manzano, Juan Francisco, *Poems by a Slave in the island of Cuba, recently liberated; translated from the Spanish by R.R. Madden, M.D., with the history of the early life of the Negro poet, written by himself,* Thomas Ward & Co., London, 1840

Mark, John, *My Trip to America and Havana in October and November 1884,* J.E. Cornish, Manchester, 1884

Murray, The Hon. Amelia, M., *Letters from the United States, Cuba and Canada,* John W. Parker & Son, London, 1856 (two volumes)

Norman, B.M., *Rambles by Land and Water or notes of travels in Cuba and Mexico,* Paine & Burgess, New York, 1845

Ogilby, John, *America: Being the Latest and most accurate description of the New World: containing the Original of the Inhabitants, and the Remarkable Voyage thither. Collected from most Authentick Authors, Augmented with later Observations, and Adorn'd with Maps and Sculptures, by John Ogilby Esq; His Majesty's Cosmographer, Geographick Printer, and Master of the Revels in the kingdom of Ireland. London, printed by the Author, and are to be had at his House in White Fryers,* 1671

Pezuela, Jacobo de la, *Historia de la Isla de Cuba,* Imprenta Española de R. Raphael, New York, 1842

Philalethes, Demoticus, *Yankee Travels through the Island of Cuba,* D. Appleton & Co., New York, 1856

Phillippo, James M., *Cuba and The United States,* Pewtress & Co., London, 1857

Rosaín, Domingo, *Necrópolis de La Habana,* Imprenta El Trabajo, Havana, 1875

Steele, James W., *Cuban Sketches,* G.P. Putnam's Sons, New York, 1881

Torre, José María de la, *Lo Que Fuimos y Lo Que Somos o La Habana Antigua y Moderna,* Imprenta de Spencer y Compañía, Havana, 1857

Wurdermann, Dr J.G.F. ('A Physician'), *Notes on Cuba,* James Munroe & Co., Boston, 1844

ACKNOWLEDGEMENTS

The author would like to thank the following organizations and individuals for permission to use photographs and illustrations:

Archivo del Museo de la cuidad de La Habana: 17 (left), 48 (below), 76, 110 (above) 172 (left), 176 (above); **Archivo General de Indias, Seville:** 20, 48 (above); **Biblioteca Nacional José Martí, Havana:** 58 (below), 81 (above right and below), 114, 134, 144 (photographs by José Ramón Fernández, Publicitur), 158, 159, 163, 172 (right), 176 (left), 178 (below left) (photograph by José Ramón Fernández, Publicitur), 190, 199 (photograph by José Ramón Fernández, Publicitur); **British Library:** 16, 17 (right), 18, 19, 22, 34, 35, 55, 77, 111, 126, 133, 138 (below), 149, 150, 155, 181, 193; **Editorial de Ciencias Sociales, La Habana** for illustrations from *Los Negros Esclavos,* Fernando Ortiz, 1987: 140, 146; **Museo de Guanabacoa:** 153 (below left); **Museo de la ciudad de La Habana:** 178 (above left and right), 187; **Museu Nacional Arte Antiga, Lisbon:** 124 (Photograph by José Pessoa, Arquivo Nacional de Fotografia, Instituto Português de Museus); **Museo Numismatico, Havana:** 32 (below right), **National Maritime Museum, Greenwich:** 47, 110 (below), 117, 118 (below); **private collection:** 106; **Wilberforce House, Hull City Museums and Art Galleries:** 138 (above).

INDEX

Page references in *italics* refer to captions to illustrations.

221

223

PRINTED IN FRANCE by Partenaires